Instant Phonics Practice

Reproducible Games, Puzzles, and Mini-Books That Target the Key Phonics Skills Beginning Readers Need to Master

LINDA WARD BEECH

New York • Toronto • London • Auckland • Sydney
Mexico City • New Delhi • Hong Kong • Buenos Aires

Teaching *Resources*

Previously published as *Fun Phonics Cut & Paste*, *Fun Phonics Mini-Books*, and *Fun Phonics Puzzles & Games*; portions revised and updated.

Cover design by Maria Lilja
Interior design by Solas
Cover and interior illustrations by Maxie Chambliss, Rusty Fletcher, and James Graham Hale.

ISBN-13: 978-0-545-13039-4
ISBN-10: 0-545-13039-5

2 3 4 5 6 7 8 9 10   40   16 15 14 13 12 11 10 09

Long Vowels

Short and Long Vowels

Rhymes and Word Families

About This Book

As children expand their literacy horizons to become readers, they need many different skills and strategies to achieve success. Among the instructional approaches that can help children unlock the mysteries of print is phonics instruction. This book includes games, puzzles, hands-on activities, and mini-books that offer practice in recognizing some of the basic sound-letter relationships children need in decoding, reading comprehension, writing, and spelling. The book is designed to engage children with hands-on activities that are lively and fun to do.

Meeting the Standards—Supporting RTI

The activities in this book also help meet key state and national language arts standards (see below), and can used to support the Response to Intervention (RTI) efforts in your school. RTI, a federal initiative, is a three-tier intervention approach in which educators provide early screening and specific, targeted intervention, particularly in reading, for students at risk. Conceived as a prevention model, the goal of RTI is to achieve success for all students. This book provides many activities for you to choose from so that you can support the varied instructional needs of your students.

Connections to the Language Arts Standards

The activities in this book support the following language arts standards for students in grades K–2, as outlined by Mid-continent Research for Education and Learning (McRel). McRel is a nationally recognized, nonprofit organization that collects and synthesizes national and state PreK–12 curriculum standards and proposes what teachers should provide for their students to grow proficient in language arts, among other curriculum areas.

Uses the general skills and strategies of the reading process including:

❖ Knows uppercase and lowercase letters of the alphabet

❖ Uses mental images based on pictures and print to aid in comprehension of text

❖ Uses basic elements of phonetic analysis (for example, common letter/sound relationships, beginning and ending consonants, vowel sounds, blends, word patterns) to decode unknown words

❖ Uses basic elements of structural analysis such as spelling patterns to decode unknown words

Source: Kendall, J. S., & Marzano, R. J. (2004). *Content knowledge: A compendium of standards and benchmarks for K–12 education.* Aurora, CO: Mid-continent Research for Education and Learning. Online database: http://www.mcrel.org/standards-benchmarks/

Management Tips

❖ To complete various activities, children will need scissors, pencils, glue sticks, crayons or colored pencils, staplers, and brass fasteners.

❖ While some children will be able to do these activities independently, others may require more help getting started. Whether you introduce the pages to individual children, small groups, or the whole class, read the instructions aloud in advance. It's also helpful to model how to complete each activity.

❖ Assist children in cutting out patterns, as needed, or do this in advance.

❖ Children can play many of the games independently. Others are more fun or work better with a partner. You may wish to pair children for different purposes.

❖ You'll find tips for specific activities, as well as the answers for each page, in the Teaching Notes that begin on page 7.

Extending Learning

❖ Build on what children have learned by extending an activity. For example:

- After completing Turn and Learn (page 48) or Make Snakes (page 90), have children use each word in a sentence. To extend At the Shop (page 82), challenge children to think of other items to add to each shop window.

- Invite children to create new activity pages based on ones in the book. They might draw and cut out new food puzzles beginning with specified letters as they did in Food Puzzles (page 37), or create new crossword puzzles for classmates to solve once they have completed Short Vowel Crosswords (page 75).

- Use Words on a Web (page 120) as a springboard for helping children make webs for other word families, as well as consonants, blends, and vowel sounds.

- Make an interactive bulletin-board center based on On the Tree (page 92). Create a multi-branched tree from brown construction paper and affix to the board at children's eye level. Choose the phonics skill you would like children to practice and gather pictures of words (from this book or old workbooks) whose names contain the target skill. Then prepare simple leaf cutouts, paste the pictures to the leaves, and place in a basket near the board. Post simple directions and invite children to visit the center in pairs or small groups and work together to tack the correct leaves to the tree.

❖ Relate the activities and mini-books to other curriculum areas. For example, you might use Tale of Tails (page 41) in a science unit on animals, while What's in the Truck? (page 86) lends itself to a unit on transportation.

❖ Each skill area includes a mini-book. Encourage children to take their mini-books home to share with their families. Place an extra copy in your classroom library. And for activity pages children are particularly proud of, you might compile send-home booklets.

❖ Work with children to create word cards from the pages they complete. Use them for word walls or place in a pocket chart so that children can look at them often as they familiarize themselves with sound-letter relationships.

Teaching Notes

On the following pages, you'll find teaching tips for completing selected pages, as well as the answers for each page.

Alphabet

page 22
Match-a-Letter Game
For this game, each pair of children will need a penny, two game markers (different-colored beans or buttons work well), and one set of uppercase letter cards (page 23).

page 24
Give a Dog a Bone!
Answers: See thumbnail of completed page at right.

Give a Dog a Bone!

page 25
ABC Picture Puzzle
Answer: Children should connect the dots to find a clown

page 26
Hidden Letter Surprise
Answer: Children should end up with the letter V.

page 27
ABC Animals
Answers: camel, dog, elephant, fish, horse, lion, octopus, pig, snake, turkey, whale, zebra

page 28
ABC Mobile
For added durability, copy the reproducible page onto cardstock, or have children use a glue stick to affix it to an old file folder before they begin cutting. Children may need help in cutting out the spiral and attaching the illustrations using tape and thin string. To hang the finished mobiles, tape a piece of string to the top of the spiral.

Answers: There are illustrations for the following 12 letters only: B–ball; G–goat; I–igloo; J–jump rope; K–kite; M–mouse; N–nest; Q–queen; R–rake; U–umbrella; V–violin; Y–yo-yo

page 29
Line Up for Lunch
Answers: Ava, Ben, Guy, Ina, Jin, Mai, Ned, Quinn, Raj, Uma, Vin, Yui

page 30
Honey Hunt
Answers: car, game, house, mitten, pen, saw, watch

Honey Hunt

Tip

Have children use a glue stick to paste the backs of the numbered pages together so that there are no blank pages in between.

page 31

Mr. A–Z's ABCs Mini-Book

Making the Mini-Books: Make a class set of the mini-book pages (pages 31–32). (You might also make an enlarged version of the book to use as a model when introducing the books to children.) Show children how to assemble their books:

1. Fold page 31 along the solid line so that the text faces out. Then fold page 32 along the solid line so that the text faces in.

2. Cut the pages apart along the dotted lines.

3. Slip pages 1 and 6 inside the cover and page 7. Then open up so that page 1 is on the left and slip in pages 2 and 5. Pages 3 and 4 go in the middle.

4. Check that the pages are in the correct order, then open to pages 3 and 4 and staple them together along the inner, center fold.

5. Invite children to color their mini-books.

Using the Mini-Books:

1. Review the letters of the alphabet with children. Have volunteers take turns pointing to various letters on a chart and identifying them.

2. Read a copy of the mini-book aloud to the class or a small group. Display the illustrations as well.

3. Talk about the story. Do children understand the significance of Mr. A–Z's name? Ask: "Why does Mr. A–Z have all the letters. Where does he keep them? Would you keep letters in these places? Why or why not?"

4. Have children read their mini-books with you. Point out that the text of the story is in speech balloons. Ask, "Who is talking in this story? Whom are they talking to?" Have children identify the letters that Mr. A–Z finds on each page.

5. Ask children what they notice about the words in the story (*They rhyme.*) Invite volunteers to identify the words that rhyme

Initial Consonants

page 33
Picture Show
Answers: B–bear K–kangaroo M–monkey T–turtle P–penguin S–seal

page 34
On the Farm
Answers: farmer, fox, fence; gate, goat, girl; jeep, jacket, jump rope

page 35
School Tools
Answers: 1. p–pencil 2. f–file folder 3. b–backpack 4. l–lunch 5. t–tape 6. c–computer 7. r–ruler 8. s–scissors

page 36
Build a House
Answers: D–door; F–fence; G–garage; M–mailbox; R–roof; W–window

page 37

Food Puzzles

Children should cut out only the puzzle parts with the dotted lines in the right column. They then match up and glue these to the puzzle parts in the left column. (Depending on children's abilities, you might want to precut the puzzle pieces.)

Answers: 1. p 2. s 3. b 4. m 5. t

page 38

Picture Books

Once children have completed the activity, let them make a cover for each of the three letter books. On each cover, have children draw another picture whose name begins with the book's letter. Children can then use their books to tell a story.

Answers: J–jump rope, jack-o-lantern; M–mouse, mop; S–sock, six

page 39

Sounds of C

Answers: Cat Box–cane, car, cup: Cent Box–celery, cereal, circus

page 40

Same Sounds

Answers: 1. pet 2. bun 3. lips 4. dig 5. rain 6. nap 7. gum 8. tops

page 41

Tale of Tails Mini-Book

Making the Mini-Books: Make a class set of the mini-book pages (pages 41–42) and the animal picture page (page 43). Set aside the picture page for use later on. (You might also make an enlarged version of the book to use as a model when introducing the book to children.) Show children how to assemble the book:

1. Fold page 41 along the solid line so that the text faces out. Then fold page 42 along the solid line so that the text faces in.
2. Cut the pages apart along the dotted lines.
3. Slip pages 1 and 6 inside the cover and page 7. Then open book so page 1 is on the left and slip in pages 2 and 5. Pages 3 and 4 go in the middle.
4. Check to be sure that the pages are in the correct order, then open to pages 3 and 4 and staple them together along the inner, center fold.

Using the Mini-Books:

1. Display the mini-book cover and read aloud the title. Talk with children about the two kinds of tales/tails mentioned in the title. Explain that this mini-book (or *tale*) has pictures of different animal *tails*, and children will be matching each tail to the correct animal to which it belongs.
2. Instruct children to look at each tail pictured in their mini-book and each animal on the picture page. When they think they know to which animal each tail belongs, have them write the letter that begins the animal name on the blank lines in the book. You might want to write the names of the animals— *kangaroo, cat, turtle, horse, pig, duck,* and *monkey*—on chart paper or a whiteboard so that children can choose among them.

Tale of Tails

Tip

Have children use a glue stick to paste the backs of the numbered pages together so that there are no blank pages in between.

3. Give each child a picture page. Have children cut out the animal pictures, glue them on the correct page in their mini-books, and then color the pictures.

4. Challenge children to think of other animals they could use to represent consonants not included in Tale of Tails (for example, a bear for *b*, or a fish for *f*). Children might then draw pictures of these animals and label them with the correct initial consonant.

Answers: 1. pig–p 2. cat–c 3. turtle–t 4. monkey–m 5. duck–d 6. kangaroo–k 7. horse–h

Final Consonants

page 44
Final Consonant Game

Children can play this game in small groups. Encourage children who are able to keep a list of the words they name.

Answers will vary.

page 45
Around the Park

For game markers, different-colored beans or buttons work well. Explain that if a player can't think of a word with the same ending sound or says an incorrect word, he or she cannot move ahead. The first player to reach Finish wins.

Answers: mop–p, leaf–f, clock–k, sun–n, dog–g, bed–d, bell–l, nest–t, ring–g, bus–s, hat–t, jam–m, car–r, crib–b. Other answers will vary.

page 46
Have a Heart

Answers: 1. vest 2. yarn 3. bib 4. stamp 5. zipper 6. seal

page 47
Hop or Run

Explain that if the picture on the card does not end with the same sound as the word a player called, then the card goes to the bottom of the pile. The winner is the player with the most cards at the end of the game.

Answers: Final p–jeep, top, clip, soap, mop, lamp, sheep; Final n–sun, pan, pen, fan, pin

page 48
Turn and Learn

Help children to align wheels 1 and 2 and secure them using a brass fastener. Challenge children to think of another picture name that ends like *wheel* and draw it in the fourth section of the wheel.

Answers: doll, pretzel, owl

page 49
What Do You See?

Remind children that each letter in the Color Code corresponds to the ending letter in each word.

Answers: The picture shows a house, trees, grass, mountains, and a sky, as follows: white house with red chimney, door, and window; black roof and path; green trees, bushes, and grass; blue sky; white mountains and smoke.

page 50
Final-Consonant Puzzle Fun

Children should cut out only the puzzle parts with the dotted lines in the right column. They then match up and glue these to the puzzle parts in the left column. (Depending on children's abilities, you might want to precut the puzzle pieces.)

Answers: 1. six 2. sun 3. flag 4. bread 5. bib

page 51
Animal Wishes Mini-Book

Making the Mini-Books: Make a class set of the mini-book pages (pages 51–53) and the picture page (page 54). Set aside the picture page for use later on. (You might also make an enlarged version of the book to use as a model when introducing the book to children.) Show children how to assemble their books:

1. Cut the pages apart along the dotted lines.

2. Arrange pages 1–11 in order, with the cover on top.

3. Staple the mini-book pages along the left side.

Using the Mini-Books:

1. Display the mini-book cover, read aloud the title, and show children the illustrations. Explain that this mini-book has pictures of different animals, each of which is wishing for something. The item they wish for ends with the same sound as the ending sound of the animal's name.

2. Read aloud the book to children, then instruct them to look at page 1 and read aloud the question. Point out the dream bubble above the toad. Explain that this is a way to show readers that a character is thinking or dreaming of something.

3. Give each child a copy of the picture page. Tell children to find the item whose name ends with the same ending sound as *Toad's* (*sled*). They then cut out the picture of the sled and glue it inside Toad's dream bubble.

4. Have children cut out the remaining pictures, glue them on the correct pages, and then color the pictures.

5. Invite children to read their completed mini-books with you. You might also ask volunteers to read their books aloud to the class.

Answers: 1. Toad–sled 2. Crab–bib 3. Pig–flag 4. Duck–book 5. Seal–bell 6. Worm–drum. 7. Hen–fan 8. Sheep–lamp 9. Bear–car 10. Octopus–bus 11. Goat–hat

Initial and Final Consonants

page 55
Two Clues
Answers: 1. cub 2. wig 3. pail 4. fox 5. log

page 56
Down the Word Steps
Answers: 1. ten 2. net 3. tub 4. bus 5. sun 6. nut 7. top 8. pan

Tip: Turn It Around
Before children begin this activity, introduce them to anagrams. Manipulate letter tiles to show them how the letters in *not*, for example, can be moved around to form *ton*.

page 57
Turn It Around
Answers: 1. bus–b, s; sub–s, b 2. tip–t, p; pit–p, t 3. ten–t, n; net–n, t 4. pot–p, t; top–t, p 5. gas–g, s; sag–s, g 6. pal–p, l; lap–l, p

page 58
Word Links
Answers: pin, n; net, t; top, p; pail, l; log, g; gas, s; sand, d; door, r; roof, f; feather

page 59
Word Chain
Help children apply a glue stick on either end of the links to form the chain.
Answers: crib, bus, sun, nail, log, gum

page 60
Nut Hunt
Explain to children that they might need to change beginning or ending letters.
Answers: 1. rug 2. tug 3. tub 4. sub 5. cub 6. cut 7. nut

page 61
Two-Way Words
Answers: 1. pop 2. dad 3. mom 4. bib 5. sis 6. Viv 7. gag 8. noon 9. wow 10. toot

page 62
Consonant Word Train Mini-Book
Making the Mini-Books: Make a class set of the mini-book and picture pages (pages 62–63). Set aside the picture page for use later on. (You might also make an enlarged version of the book to use as a model when introducing the book to children.) Show children how to assemble their books:

1. Cut the pages apart along the dotted lines.

2. Beginning with the engine and ending with the caboose, show children how to tape the train cars together in order.

Using the Mini-Books:
1. Display the mini-book cover (the train engine), read aloud the title, and ask children to identify the illustration (*pen*).

2. Give each child a copy of the picture page. Tell children to find a picture whose name begins with the same ending sound as *pen* (*nest*). Have them cut out the picture of the nest and glue it to the train car right behind the engine.

Consonant Word Train

3. Explain that the next train car should have a picture whose name begins with the ending sound in *nest*–t. Let children search for the picture of the tub and glue it in place.

4. Have children then cut out the remaining pictures and glue them on the correct train cars following the same procedure. The last page (the caboose) has a picture of a lion whose initial letter corresponds with the last letter of the word in number 6 (*girl*).

5. Invite children to color the pictures and then accordion-fold the pages so that the cover is on top.

Answers: 1. nest 2. tub 3. bus 4. soap 5. pig 6. girl

Consonant Blends
page 64
Color-the-Blends Puzzle
Answers: Children should color the hot-air balloon scene as follows: sky, blue; buildings and dog, brown; hill, green; balloon basket, yellow; balloon: red, purple, and green.

page 65
New Words
Answers: 1. tray–t 2. clock–c 3. glove–g 4. swing–s 5. flag–f 6. broom–b 7. drip–d 8. plate–p

page 66
Who Am I?
Answers: 1. snake 2. frog 3. skunk 4. fly 5. crab 6. swan

page 67
Picture Words
You may wish to explain that the new words represented by the pictures are called compound words because they are made from two words put together.

Answers: 1. dragonfly 2. skateboard 3. starfish 4. sunflower 5. nutcracker

page 68
On the Chart
Answers: br–bride, brush, bread, bridge; st–step, stamp, star, stove; cl–clock, cloud, clown, claw

page 69
Picture Perfect
Answers: 1. crown 2. bridge 3. skateboard 4. blanket 5. tree

page 70
Slide the Letters
Help children cut the slits in the patterns and then slip the letter strips through the slits. Demonstrate how to move the letter strips to form words.

Answers: op–stop, clop, plop, drop, crop, flop; ow–snow, stow, blow, grow, slow, flow

Tips: Slide the Letters
- Enlarge the patterns, if desired.
- For added durability, copy the reproducible page onto cardstock or have children use a glue stick to affix it to an old file folder before cutting.
- To keep the strips from slipping out of the slits, fold a piece of tape, wider than the strips, over the ends.
- For added fun, give each child a craft stick to tape to the back of the stop sign, making sure not to tape over the slit.

My l-Blend Wheel

page 71

___ -Blend Wheel Mini-Book

Making the Mini-Books: For each wheel book, make a class set of the cover wheel (page 71) and Wheels 1, 2, and 3 (pages 72–74). Set aside Wheels 2 and 3 for use later on. (You might wish to make an enlarged version of each wheel book to use as a model when introducing the books to children.) Show children how to assemble the Wheel 1 book:

1. Cut out the cover wheel and Wheel 1 along the dotted lines.

2. Cut out the pie-shaped window on the cover wheel.

3. Color the pictures on Wheel 1.

4. Insert a brass fastener through the center of the cover to attach Wheel 1.

Using the Mini-Books:

1. Begin by reviewing l-blends with the class. Give examples such as *fl/flock, cl/ clay, bl/blue, pl/plow,* and *gl/glad.*

2. Show children how to hold the cover wheel in one hand and turn the bottom wheel with the other. Have children identify the pictures and read the words on the wheel. Ask children what the words have in common (they all contain the l-blend). Have children then fill in the blend on the line on the cover.

3. Invite volunteers to use each blend word in a complete sentence. Encourage them to think of other l-blend words, too.

4. Provide children with fresh cover wheels to assemble wheels 2 and 3. Have them follow the same procedure to practice *r*-blend and *s*-blend words.

Short Vowels

page 75
Short Vowel Crosswords
Answers: 1. I–WIG, PIN 2. U–TUB, CUP 3. E–HEN, BED 4. O–TOP, FOX 5. A–FAN, BAT

page 76
Short Vowel Banners
Punch holes in the top corners of the banners and attach yarn to hang them.

Answers: short a–bat, cat, pan; short o–clock, frog, mop

page 77
Short Vowel Tic-Tac-Toe
Tell children that they can go across, down, or diagonally to find a row.

Answers: 1. short a–hat, mask, can 2. short i–milk, pin, pig 3. short e–pen, bed, sled

page 78
Short Vowel Animals
Answers: 1. E–HEN 2. I–PIG 3. A–CRAB 4. U–PUP 5. O–FROG

page 79
Bunny Hop
Show children how to fold the tab under the bunny so it can stand on each picture as they read along. Explain to children that they can glue the pictures on the path in any order as long as the picture names have the short-*u* sound.

Answers: duck, cup, rug, bus, tub, gum, bug

page 80
Letter Windows
Help children cut the slits in the hat and rug and guide them in slipping the letter strips through the slits. Demonstrate how to move the letter strips to form words.

Answers: -at–hat, fat, cat, sat, mat, pat; -ug–rug, hug, bug, tug, jug, mug

page 81
Who Did It?
Answers: 1. duck 2. cat 3. pig 4. fox 5. hen 6. nest. Children should draw a hen using a hat as a nest.

page 82
At the Shop
Answers: short e–sled, tent; short i–bib, ring; short u–mug, truck

page 83
Toss and Tell
Have children cut out the cube pattern along the dotted lines, fold along the solid lines, and assemble using a glue stick or tape. Children can play until they have checked all of the words or until they've checked at least one word with each short vowel. If children play with a partner, they can each use a different-colored crayon to keep track of the words they check.

Answers: lamp–cab, at, ham; dress–sled, egg, vest; box–top, hog, hot; brush–rug, bug, mud; sink–pig, win, hill

page 84
Sentence Fun
Check that children understand that the word they add to each sentence must make sense as well as match the short vowel sound.

Answers: 1. hat 2. pet 3. tub 4. dish 5. sad 6. yet

page 85
That Cat
Show children how to fold the tab under the cat so it can stand on each picture as they read along.

Answers: 1. bus 2. wig 3. lamp 4. box 5. bed

page 86
What's in the Truck? Mini-Book
Making the Mini-Books: Make a class set of the mini-book pages (pages 86–89). You might also make an enlarged version of the book to use as a model when introducing the book to children. Show children how to assemble their books:

Tips: Letter Windows
• Enlarge the patterns if desired.
• For added durability, copy the reproducible page onto cardstock or have children use a glue stick to affix it to an old file folder before cutting.
• To keep the strips from slipping out of the slits, fold a piece of tape, wider than the strips, over the ends.

1. Cut out the truck shape and the six book pages.

2. Arrange them in order with the cover on top.

3. Staple the pages together along the top edge, and then affix them to the truck by gluing the back of the last page to the truck.

Using the Mini-Books:

1. Begin by reviewing the short vowel sounds with the class. Give examples of one-syllable words with each sound, for example, *ham, ten, lid, dot,* and *bus.*

2. Show children your copy of the mini-book, pointing out how the base of the book is in the shape of a truck while the pages lift up. Discuss the short vowel sound featured on each page and have children identify the pictures.

3. Have children turn to page 1 of their books. Encourage them to think of other words that have the short-*a* sound. List the words that can be easily illustrated on chart paper or a whiteboard. Then invite children to draw their own picture.

4. Have children continue this process with the remaining mini-book pages. Invite them to share their pictures, using complete sentences to describe them. Then have children color the pictures in their books.

Answers will vary.

Tip
Make a large chart or word wall listing all of the words from the truck books that illustrate each of the short vowel sounds.

Long Vowels

page 90
Make Snakes
Answers: Children should paste a snake body to the heads in: 1. frame 3. rake 4. skate 6. plane.

page 91
Animal Crossword
Answers: See crossword at left.

Animal Crossword

page 92
On the Tree
Answers: bee, jeep, sheep, seal, wheel

page 93
Picture Maze
Answers: gate, cane, game, rake, tray, vane, tape, plane, mane, cake, hay, cape, snake, nail, snail, train, chain, whale, vase, pail

page 94
Long-i Cut and Paste
Answers: slide, bride, tie, ice, nine, kite

page 95
Grid Game
Before children begin, you may wish to introduce or review the use of grids. For example, to find the point A, 2, start at the letter A on the left and trace a path with a finger to the picture of the bee, located where line 2 intersects with line A.

Answers: 1. bee 2. deer 3. zebra 4. sheep 5. seal 6. eel. All share the long-e sound.

page 96

Ghost Questions

Answers: 1. robe 2. snow 3. soap 4. nose 5. phone 6. boat

page 97

U Stew

Answers: ruler, tube, glue, flute

page 98

Whale Tale

Answers: 1. pie 2. seal 3. rose 4. flute 5. plane

page 99

Changes

Answers: 1. pole 2. vane 3. mule 4. boat 5. bike 6. rose

page 100

Riddle Fun

Answers: 1. <u>snow</u>ball, fill-in-the-blanks: <u>s</u>oap, <u>sn</u>ail, b<u>o</u>ne, <u>wh</u>eel
2. <u>time</u>, fill-in-the-blanks: goa<u>t</u>, br<u>i</u>de, <u>m</u>ice, tre<u>e</u>.

page 101

Colors Around the Year Mini-Book

Making the Mini-Books: Make a class set of the mini-book pages and word strip (pages 101–102). Set aside the word strip for use later on. (You might also make an enlarged version of the book to use as a model when introducing the book to children.) Show children how to assemble their books:

1. Cut the pages apart along the dotted lines.

2. Arrange pages 1–5 in order with the cover on top.

3. Staple the mini-book pages along the left side.

Using the Mini-Books:

1. Begin by reviewing the long vowel sounds with the class. Give examples of one-syllable words with each sound, for example, *lake, team, mice, boat,* and *glue.*

2. Display the mini-book cover, read aloud the title, and ask children to identify what's happening in the illustrations.

3. Read aloud your copy of the mini-book, drawing children's attention to the long vowel hint and illustration shown on each page.

4. Give each child a copy of the word strip, review the words, and ask children to identify the long vowel sound in each word.

5. Instruct children to turn to page 1 of their books. Together, read the text and talk about the colors of leaves in the fall. Then have children look at the word strip. Ask: "What long vowel word best completes the sentence? (*gold*) Tell children to cut and paste the word on the line provided.

6. Have children continue using the clues to fill in the remaining mini-book pages. Once they have placed all the color words correctly, invite them to use crayons in corresponding colors to color the illustrations.

Answers: 1. gold 2. gray 3. white 4. green 5. blue

Tips: U Stew

• Help children cut the slits along the dotted lines in the pot and then show them how to tuck the tabs on the pictures into the slits.

• To keep the pictures in place, children can dab a glue stick on the tabs after inserting in the slits.

Short and Long Vowels

page 103
Wrong One Game
Answers: 1. Replace *tray* with *seal*. 2. Replace *soap* with *cake*. 3. Replace *chick* with *ten*. 4. Replace *sock* with *skunk*.

page 104
Train Ride
Answers: long-a train–tray, rake, vase, pail; short-a train–crab, hat, stamp, can

page 105
What's Missing?
Answers: Children should draw the following: 1. road 2. bat 3. wheel 4. bed 5. kite

page 106
Short and Long
Answers: 1. van 2. cube 3. pin 4. cape 5. tub 6. robe 7. cane 8. mop

page 107
Name the Vowels
Model how to make and use a spinner using a large paper clip and a pencil.

Answers: long vowel words–tree, stove, game, leaf, glue, paint, goat, tie, slide; short vowel words–mop, flag, truck, net, crib, bus.

page 108
Vowel Tic-Tac-Toe
Tell children that they can go across, down, or diagonally to find a row.

Answers: 1. short e–fence, bed, ten 2. long i–kite, nine, dice
3. short u–jump, nut, lunch 4. long o–rope, soap, coat

page 109
Road Race Game
Have children color their cars differently so they can keep track of them.

Answers: long e–heel; long a–stain, hay, frame; long i–five, pie, ice, dime; long o–rose; long u–tube; short e–shell, wet, sled; short a–cap, sad; short i–fish; short o–clock, hop; short u–duck, mug

page 110
Vowel Opposites
You may wish to review opposites with children before giving them this activity.

Answers: 1. in 2. play 3. shut 4. hot 5. you 6. mad 7. sleep 8. white 9. go 10. men

page 111
Number Match-Up
Answers: 1. three 2. five 3. six 4. ten 5. nine

page 112
Color Clues

Before children begin, explain that many color names have either a long or short vowel sound. Write the following words on chart paper or a whiteboard and review the vowel sound for each word: *pink, gray, red, green, black, blue*.

Answers: 1. black 2. pink 3. green 4. blue 5. red 6. gray

page 113
Going to Work Mini-Book

Making the Mini-Books: Make a class set of the mini-book pages (pages 113–115) and the picture page (page 116). Set aside the picture page for use later on. (You might also make an enlarged version of the book to use as a model when introducing the book to children.) Show children how to assemble their books:

1. Cut out the briefcase shapes along the dotted lines.

2. Arrange the five mini-book pages in order with the cover on top.

3. Staple the mini-book pages along the handle (the top edge).

Using the Mini-Books:

1. Begin by reading aloud the title of the mini-book and asking children to identify the items shown on the cover. Encourage them to tell the short or long vowel sound for each. Explain that this book has pictures of things that people might take to a job in an office. The items begin with short and long vowel sounds.

2. Read aloud the book to children. Draw their attention to the two sections of each mini-book page; one is for short vowel words and the other for long vowel words. Have children identify the pictures and the vowel sounds on each page.

3. Give each child a copy of the picture page. Have children cut out the pictures. Read aloud each picture name and have children identify the vowel sound for each.

4. Read aloud the text on page 1. Explain that children should find a picture of something whose name has the short-*a* sound for the first sentence and a picture of something whose name has the long-*a* sound for the second.

5. Have children then cut out the remaining pictures, glue them on the correct pages, and then color the pictures.

6. Invite children to read their completed mini-books with you. You might also ask volunteers to read their books aloud to the class.

Answers: 1. short a–hat, long a–tape 2. short o–clock, long o–comb 3. short i–clips, long i–dime 4. short e–thread, long e–key 5. short u–mug, long u–glue

Rhymes and Word Families
page 117
Rhymes and Shapes

Answers: 1. back 2. get 3. hot 4. lid 5. pump 6. tap

page 118
Word Family Flowers

Answers: van–fan, can, man; bug–mug, jug, rug

page 119
Rhyme Roll Game

Suggest that children write down the words they say so that they don't reuse them.

Answers will vary.

page 120
Words on a Web

Answers: 1–8. bit, fit, hit, kit, lit, pit, sit, wit

page 121
Fat Cat Game

Model the game for children before they play and share these playing tips:

- Remind children that rhyming words often belong to the same word family. For example, the words in *fat cat* belong to the *–at* word family. This means that the second and third letter in each word will always be the same. This will help them narrow down their guesses.

- If a player guesses a letter that appears in both words of the rhyme, for example, *a* and *t*, the letters should be written in both words at that time. However, children may draw only one body part for each new correct letter they name. In this example, they could draw the first ear for naming *a* and the second ear for *t*.

- You might suggest that children draw the cat in this order: first ear, second ear, body, tail.

- Instead of drawing their cats on the activity page, you might have children use separate sheets of paper.

page 122
Rhyme Flip-Ups

Check that children glue only the tab at the top of each picture so that they can lift the pictures to see the rhyming words.

Answers: 1. tag 2. bell 3. sun 4. bed 5. pin 6. bus

page 123
Rhyme Find

Answers: 1. well 2. snail 3. hug 4. block 5. bat

Rhyme Hunt

page 124
Rhyme Hunt

Children might use different-colored crayons to highlight the words in each word family.

page 125
Silly Sock Rhymes

Answers: left to right—map, cap; tub, sub; big, pig; hen, men; bell, tell

page 126
Make It Rhyme
Instead of drawing in the blank boxes, you might have children draw their pictures on separate sheets of paper.

Answers: 1. slide 2. peach 3. street 4. play 5. blue

page 127
Rhyme Time Mini-Book
Making the Mini-Book: Make a class set of the mini-book pages (pages 127–128). You might also make an enlarged version of the book to use as a model when introducing the book to children. Show children how to assemble their books:

1. Cut apart the cover and page 7 (the picture page) and set aside.

2. Fold the remaining part of page 127 along the solid line so that the text faces out. Then fold page 128 along the solid line so that the text faces in.

3. Cut the folded pages on page 128 apart along the dotted lines.

4. Slip pages 2 and 5 inside pages 1 and 6. Then slip pages 3 and 4 in the middle.

5. Check that the pages are in the correct order, place the cover on top, and then staple them together on the left.

Tip
Have children use a glue stick to paste the backs of the numbered pages together so that there are no blank pages in between.

Using the Mini-Books:

1. Begin by reviewing the short vowel sounds with the class. Give examples of one-syllable words with each sound, for example, *sat, ten, rink, pop,* and *tug.*

2. Display the mini-book cover, read aloud the title, and ask children to identify what is happening in the illustrations. Then ask them what they notice about the words. (*They rhyme.*)

3. Read your copy of the mini-book aloud to the class or a small group, displaying the illustrations and pointing out the rhyming words on each page.

4. Instruct children to turn to page 1 of their books. Together read the text and ask children to identify the rhyming words (*Jan* and *pan*).

5. Have children look at the pictures on the picture page (page 7). Then ask: "What picture best completes the sentence?" (*fan*) Have children cut out the picture of the fan and glue it in the box on page 1. Then encourage them to write the word on the lines provided, one letter per line.

6. Have children continue using the rhyming verses to complete the remaining mini-book pages, and then have them color their books.

7. Challenge children to think of other rhyming words they could use on each page of their book.

Answers: 1. fan 2. pen 3. swing 4. trunk 6. shop

Name _____

Match-a-Letter Game

Players: 2

1. Take turns tossing a penny.
   - If it lands 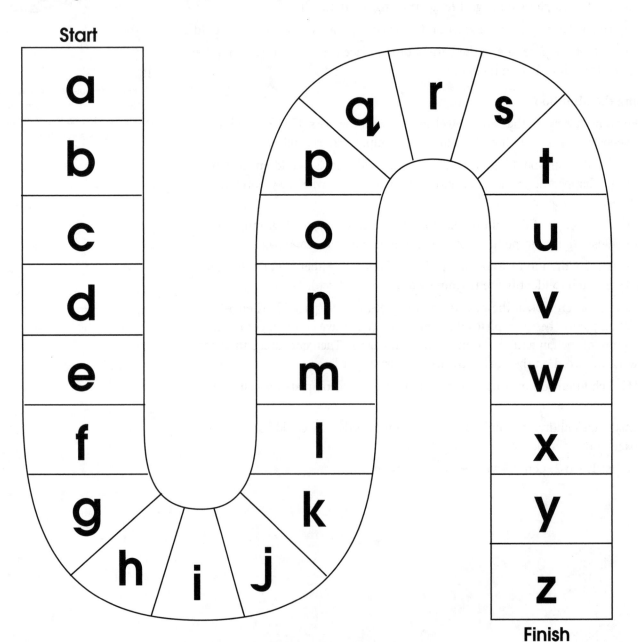, move 1 space.
   - If it lands , move 2 spaces.

2. What lowercase letter did you land on?
   Find the uppercase letter that matches.

3. The game ends when both players reach Finish.

Start

a
b
c
d
e
f
g
h i j k l m n o p
q r s t
u
v
w
x
y
z

Finish

A B C D E

F G H I J

K L M N O

P Q R S T

U V W X Y

Z

Match-a-Letter Game Letters

Name _____

Give a Dog a Bone!

1. Read the lowercase letters on each bone.
2. Read the uppercase letters on the dogs.
3. Cut and paste each bone near its matching dog.

 ABC

 DEF

 GHI

 JKL

 MNO

 PQR

 STU

 VWX

 YZ

| stu | def | pqr | yz |
| abc | jkl | vwx | ghi | mno |

Instant Phonics Practice © 1999, 2009 Linda Ward Beech, Scholastic Teaching Resources

Name _____

ABC Picture Puzzle

1. Find the hidden picture!
Connect the dots in ABC order.

2. Tell a story about the picture.

Name _____

Hidden Letter Surprise

Color the squares in ABC order.
• You can go across, down, and up.
• The squares you color must touch.
What letter does the pattern make?

A	B	W	T	H	X	P	Z	D	M	Y	A	Y	Z
K	C	D	M	Q	S	W	Z	J	T	L	W	X	T
B	L	E	F	Y	C	F	R	N	D	U	V	J	C
S	X	R	G	H	P	T	V	C	S	T	O	K	E
C	U	N	A	I	J	Y	B	Q	R	Z	N	A	K
E	K	X	W	C	K	L	O	P	D	O	G	Q	I
V	J	D	L	E	S	M	N	V	A	S	U	L	B

Instant Phonics Practice © 1999, 2009 Linda Ward Beech, Scholastic Teaching Resources

Name _____

ABC Animals

1. Say each animal name.
Listen for the beginning sound.

2. Cut and paste the animals along the stone path
in ABC order.

3. Write the letter that stands for the beginning sound
below each stone.

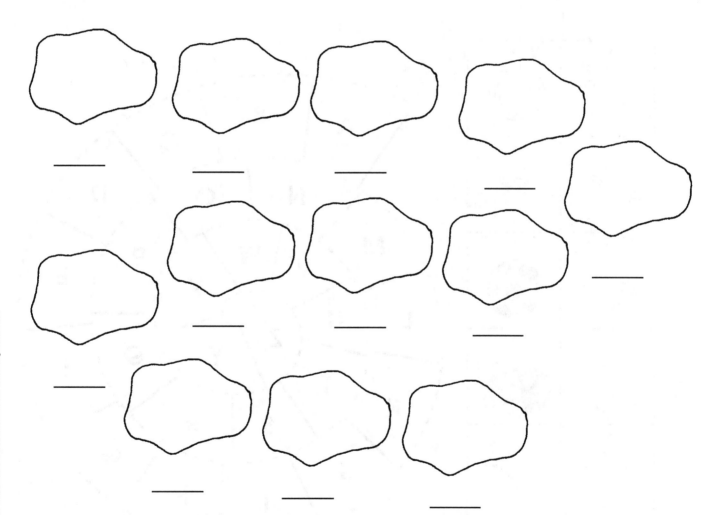

Name _____

ABC Mobile

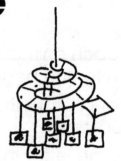

1. Say each picture name.
Listen for the beginning sound.

2. Make a mobile!
Cut out the pictures and the spiral.

3. Hang the pictures along the spiral in ABC order.

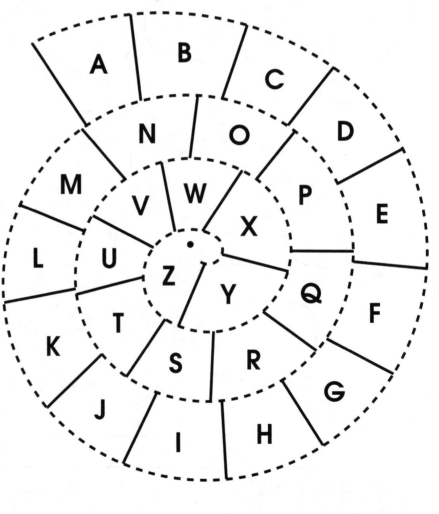

Name _____

Line Up for Lunch

1. Look at each child's name.

2. What letter does each name start with?

3. Cut and paste the faces on the lunch line in ABC order.

Start   **Finish**

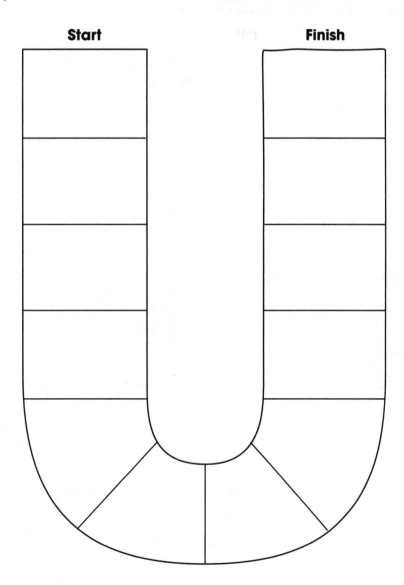

 **Guy**   **Uma**   **Ned**   **Jin**   **Yui**   **Mai**

 **Vin**   **Raj**   **Ina**   **Ava**   **Quinn**   **Ben**

Name _____

Honey Hunt

1. Help Bear find the honey.
What letter does each picture name start with?

2. Draw a path for Bear.
Follow pictures on the path in ABC order.

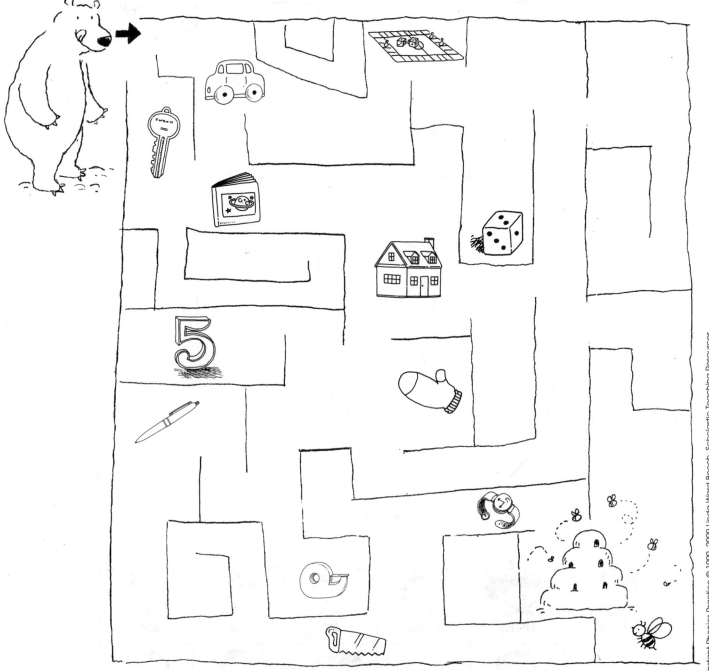

Instant Phonics Practice © 1999, 2009 Linda Ward Beech, Scholastic Teaching Resources

Four more letters and we're done.
Mr. A–Z, your game is fun.
Now we'll learn and not forget
the letters of the alphabet.

7

Mr. A–Z's ABCs Mini-Book, page 31

Mr. A–Z's ABCs

P, Q, and R must be here, too.
Mr. A–Z, it's up to you.

5

Instant Phonics Practice © 1999, 2009 Linda Ward Beech, Scholastic Teaching Resources

Thank you, but we need more.
Are there letters in the drawer?

2

1

Mr. A-Z's ABCs Mini-Book, page 32

6

3

Instant Phonics Practice © 1999, 2009 Linda Ward Beech, Scholastic Teaching Resources

4

Name _____

Picture Show

1. Say each animal name.
Listen for the beginning sound.

2. Cut and paste each animal in the
with the letter that stands for its beginning sound.

Name _____

On the Farm

1. Look at the scene.

2. Find pictures whose names begin with **f**, **g**, or **j**.

3. Write the correct letter on each line.

4. Then color the scene.

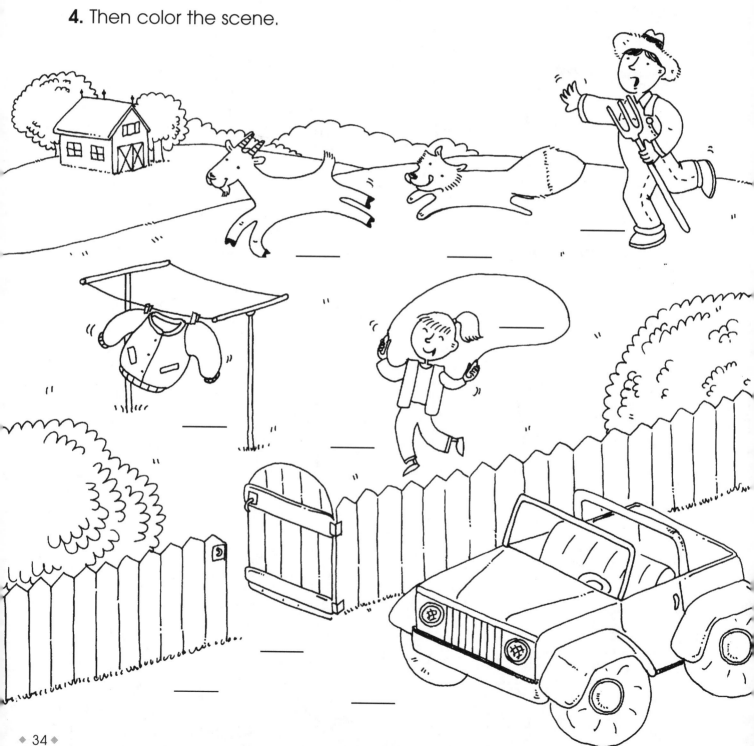

Name _____

School Tools

1. Name each school tool.

2. Write the letter that each tool's name begins with.

1.  _____

2.  _____

3. 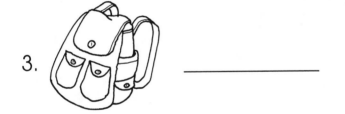 _____

4. 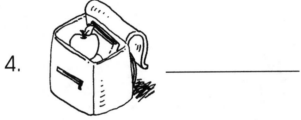 _____

5. 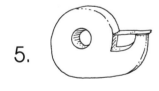 _____

6.  _____

7.  _____

8.  _____

Name _____

Build a House

1. Say each picture name.
Listen for the beginning sound.

2. What letter stands for each sound?

3. Cut and paste the pictures to match each letter.

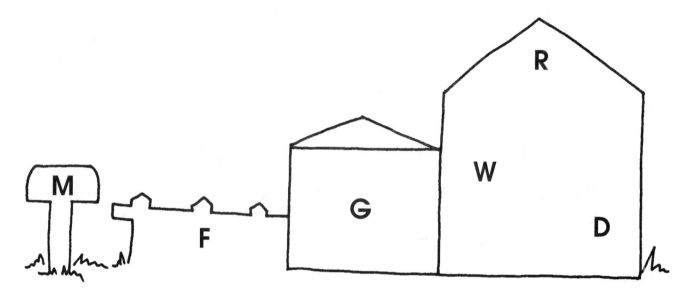

Instant Phonics Practice © 1999, 2009 Linda Ward Beech, Scholastic Teaching Resources

Name _____

Food Puzzles

1. Say the name of each food.
Listen for the beginning sound.

2. What letter stands for each sound?

3. Put the puzzle parts together.
Cut and paste the letters to match the pictures.

1.    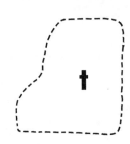 **s**

2.    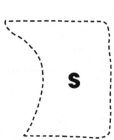 **m**

3. 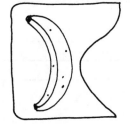   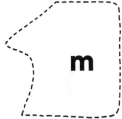 **t**

4. 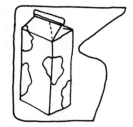    **p**

5.    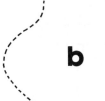 **b**

Name _____

Picture Books

1. Say each picture name.
   Listen for the beginning sound.
2. What letter on the books stands for each sound?
3. Cut out the pictures and the books.
4. Paste each picture on the correct letter book.

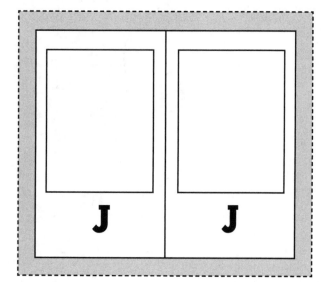

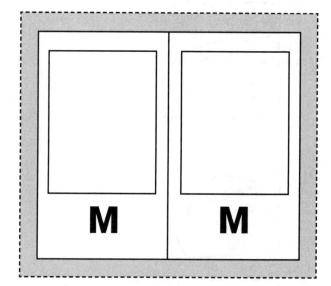

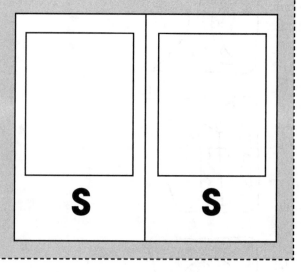

Instant Phonics Practice © 1999, 2009 Linda Ward Beech, Scholastic Teaching Resources

Name _____

Sounds of C

1. Say each picture name.
Listen for the sound of the letter **C**.
at the beginning of each word. It will either be
a hard **C** like 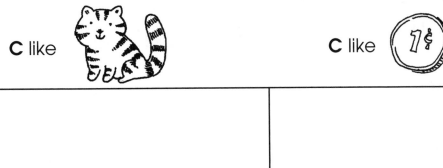 or a soft **C** like ⓣ.

2. Cut and paste the pictures in the boxes.
- Paste pictures that begin like "cat" in the 🐱 box.
- Paste pictures that begin like "cent" in the ⓣ box.

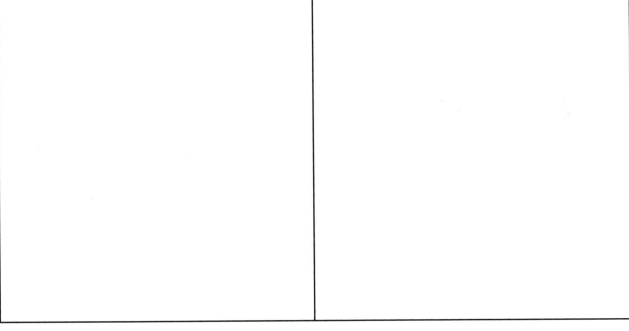

C like   **C** like

Name _____

Same Sounds

1. Look at the underlined words in each sentence.

2. Say the beginning sound.

3. Find a word at the bottom of the page
that begins with the same sound.

4. Finish the sentences. Cut and paste the words
with the same beginning letter sound into the boxes.

1. <u>Pam</u> <u>picks</u> a [＿＿＿] .

2. <u>Bob</u> <u>bit</u> a [＿＿＿] .

3. <u>Len</u> <u>licked</u> his [＿＿＿] .

4. <u>Did</u> the <u>dog</u> [＿＿＿] ?

5. The <u>rat</u> <u>runs</u> in the [＿＿＿] .

6. <u>Nan</u> <u>needs</u> a [＿＿＿] .

7. The <u>girl</u> <u>got</u> some [＿＿＿] .

8. <u>Ted</u> has <u>ten</u> [＿＿＿] .

nap	pet	rain	tops
gum	lips	bun	dig

Instant Phonics Practice © 1999, 2009 Linda Ward Beech, Scholastic Teaching Resources

_____

Tale of Tails

Tale of Tails Mini-Book, page 41

_____

Instant Phonics Practice © 1999, 2009 Linda Ward Beech, Scholastic Teaching Resources

_____

1

_____

3

_____

6

_____

4

_____

Tale of Tails Mini-Book Pictures

Name _____

Final Consonant Game

Players: 1 or 2

1. Toss a penny on the game board.
What letter did it land on?

2. Say a word that ends with that letter's sound.

3. How many different words can you name?

G	S	L	D
B	P	K	N
F	R	T	M

Instant Phonics Practice © 1999, 2009 Linda Ward Beech, Scholastic Teaching Resources

Name _____

Around the Park

Players: 2

1. Toss a penny into the number box.
   - Did it land on 1? Move 1 space.
   - Did it land on 2? Move 2 spaces.

2. Say the picture name on the space.

3. What sound does it end with?
   Say a word with the same ending sound.

1	2

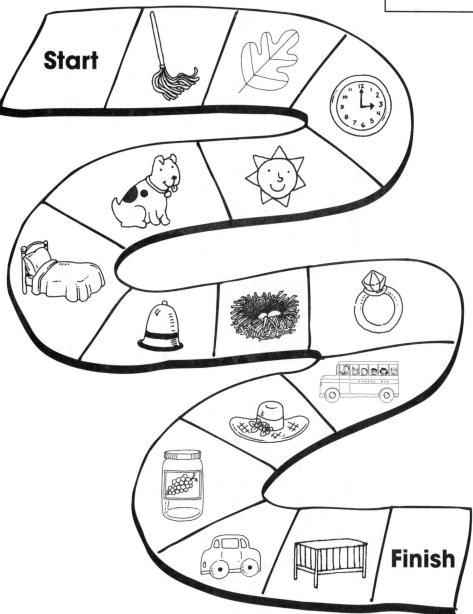

Name _____

Have a Heart

1. Say each picture name on the hearts.

2. What picture name at the bottom of the page ends with the same sound?

3. Cut and paste the picture with the same ending sound on the other side of each heart.

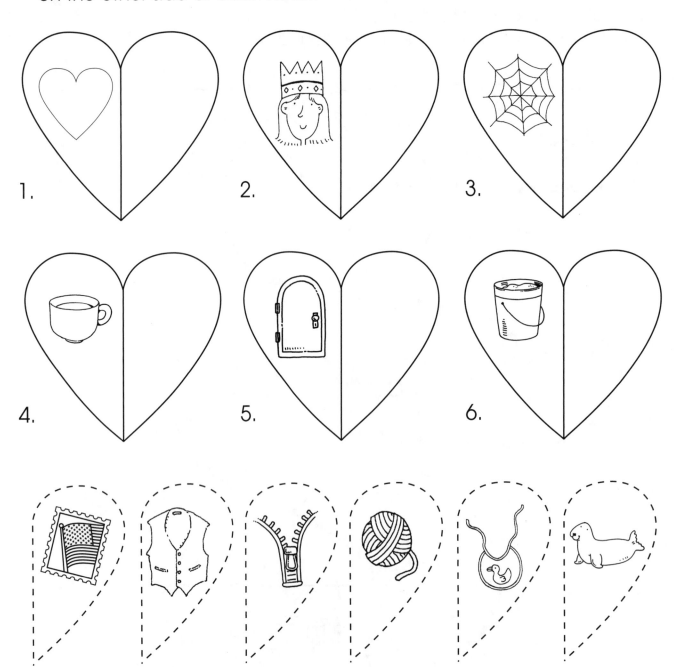

Name _____

Hop or Run

Players: 2

1. Cut out the cards. Stack them facedown.

2. Say the word "hop" or the word "run."

3. Then pick a card. Does the picture name end
with the same sound (**p** or **n**) as the word you called?
• If so, keep the card.
• If not, put the card at the bottom of the stack.

4. Take turns until all the cards are taken.
The player with the most cards wins.

Name _____

Turn and Learn

1. Say each picture name.

2. Do any of the picture names have
the same ending sound as "wheel"?
If so, cut and paste them on wheel 2.

3. Cut out both wheels.
Use a 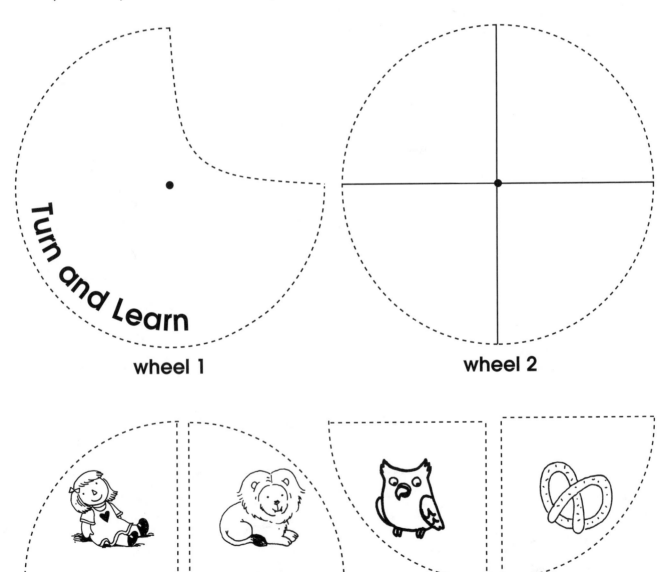 to put them together.

4. Say each picture name as you turn the wheel.

Turn and Learn

wheel 1

wheel 2

Name _____

What Do You See?

1. Say the words.
Listen for the ending sounds.

2. Use the Ending-Sounds Color Code
to make a picture.

Ending-Sounds Color Code				
s = blue	t = green	d = black	l = red	m = white

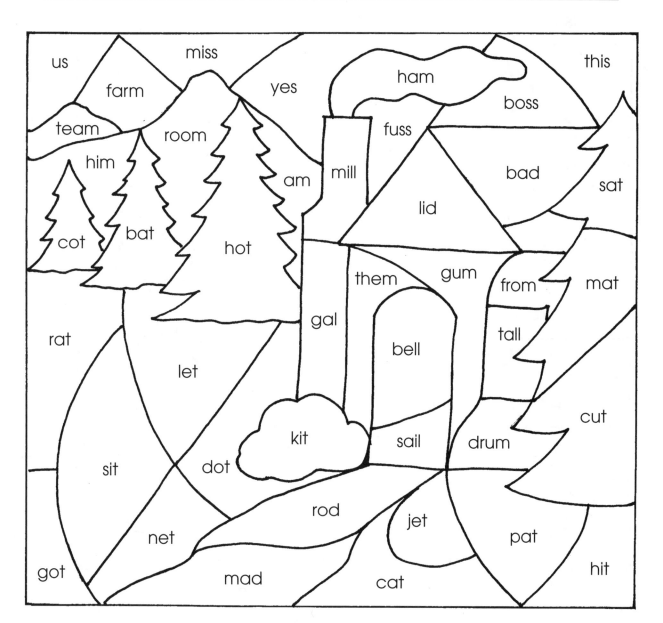

Name _____

Final-Consonant Puzzle Fun

Cut and paste the puzzle parts to match each clue.

1. It ends like

2. It ends like

3. It ends like

4. It ends like

   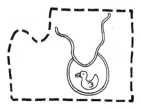

5. It ends like

Instant Phonics Practice © 1999, 2009 Linda Ward Beech, Scholastic Teaching Resources

Animal Wishes

What does Toad wish for?

Animal Wishes Mini-Book, page 51

1

What does Crab wish for?

Instant Phonics Practice © 1999, 2009 Linda Ward Beech, Scholastic Teaching Resources

What does Pig wish for?

What does Duck wish for?

4

What does Seal wish for?

5

What does Worm wish for?

6

What does Hen wish for?

7

What does Sheep wish for?

8

Animal Wishes Mini-Book, page 53

What does Bear wish for?

9

What does Octopus wish for?

10

Instant Phonics Practice © 1999, 2009 Linda Ward Beech, Scholastic Teaching Resources

What does Goat wish for?

11

Animal Wishes Mini-Book Pictures

Instant Phonics Practice © 1999, 2009 Linda Ward Beech, Scholastic Teaching Resources

Name _____

Two Clues

Cut and paste the pictures to match each clue.

1. It begins like and ends like  .

2. It begins like  and ends like .

3. It begins like and ends like .

4. It begins like and ends like  .

5. It begins like  and ends like  .

Name _____

Down the Word Steps

1. Work your way down the word steps.
Follow the clues and fill in each crossword.

(The last letter of each word
is the first letter of a new word.)

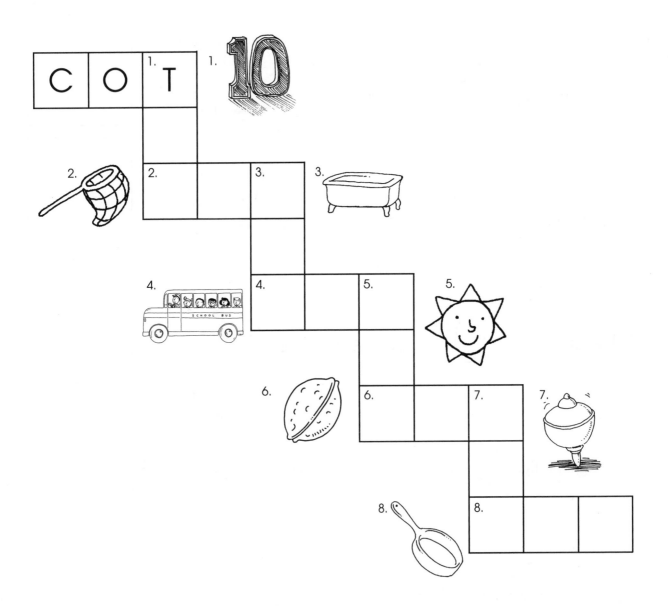

Instant Phonics Practice © 1999, 2009 Linda Ward Beech, Scholastic Teaching Resources

Name _____

Turn It Around

1. Cut out the words at the bottom of the page.

2. Paste each word in the box below the word
that has the same letters but are switched around.

3. What letter stands for the beginning sound of each word?

4. What letter stands for the ending sound?

5. Write the letters on the lines.

	Beginning Sound	Ending Sound
1. bus	_____	_____
	_____	_____
2. tip	_____	_____
	_____	_____
3. ten	_____	_____
	_____	_____
4. pot	_____	_____
	_____	_____
5. gas	_____	_____
	_____	_____
6. pal	_____	_____
	_____	_____

top   net   sag   lap   sub   pit

Name _____

Word Links

1. Write the letter for the ending sound
of each word in the ◯ that's next to it.

2. Then find the picture at the bottom
of the page that begins with that same ending sound.
Each new word will begin with the ending sound
of the word that comes before it.

3. Paste it in the ☐. The first one has been done for you.

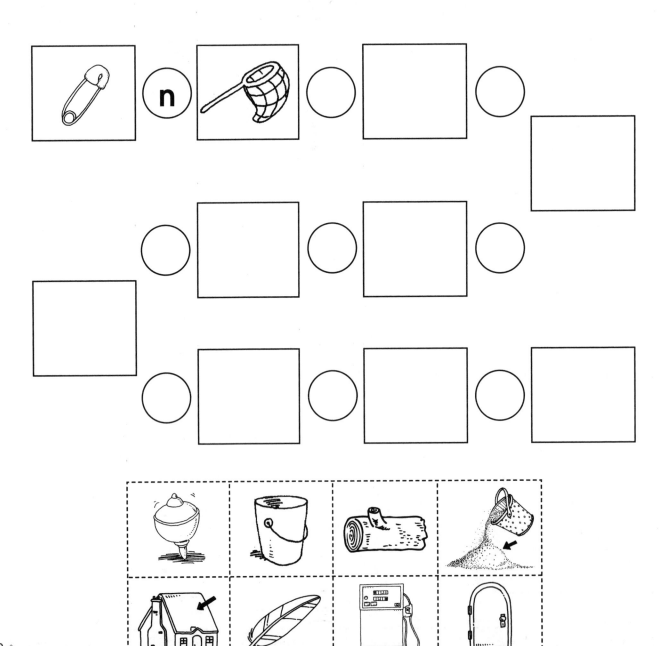

Instant Phonics Practice © 1999, 2009 Linda Ward Beech, Scholastic Teaching Resources

Name _____

Word Chain

1. Cut out the strips along the dotted lines.

2. Make a word chain. Start with "crib."

3. Each word in the chain begins with the last letter of the word before it.

paste

gum

bus

crib

nail

sun

log

paste

Instant Phonics Practice © 1999, 2009 Linda Ward Beech, Scholastic Teaching Resources

Name _____

Nut Hunt

1. Help Sammy find a nut. Start with the word "bug."
   Then follow the clues to make new words.

2. Paste a picture to show what each new word is.

Clue	Word	Picture

b   u   g

1. Change **b** to **r**   ___ ___ ___

2. Change **r** to **t**   ___ ___ ___

3. Change **g** to **b**   ___ ___ ___

4. Change **t** to **s**   ___ ___ ___

5. Change **s** to **c**   ___ ___ ___

6. Change **b** to **t**   ___ ___ ___

7. Change **c** to **n**   ___ ___ ___

Instant Phonics Practice © 1999, 2009 Linda Ward Beech, Scholastic Teaching Resources

Name _____

Two-Way Words

1. Cut out the letters at the bottom of the page.
2. Paste them so that each word begins
   and ends with the same sound.

1. po _____

6. Vi _____

2. da _____

7. ga _____

3. mo _____

8. noo _____

4. bi _____

9. wo _____

5. si _____

10. too _____

b	t	d	m	s
p	g	n	w	v

Consonant Word Train

1

2

3

4

5

6

7

Instant Phonics Practice © 1999, 2009 Linda Ward Beech, Scholastic Teaching Resources, Consonant Word Train Mini-Book, page 62

Consonant Word Train Mini-Book Pictures

Name _____

Color-the-Blends Puzzle

1. Say the words.
Listen for the beginning sounds.

2. Use the Consonant-Blends Color Code
to make a picture.

Consonant-Blends Color Code					
bl = blue	cl = red	fl = yellow	gl = green	pl = brown	sl = purple

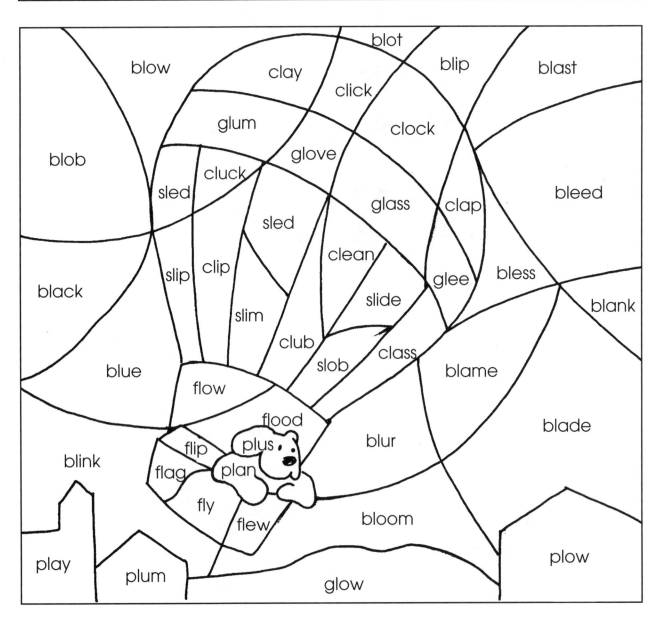

Name _____

New Words

1. Cut out the letters at the bottom of the page.
2. Paste a letter to change each word.
   Use the picture clues to help you.

1. Change **ray** to _____ ray

2. Change **lock** to _____ lock

3. Change **love** to _____ love

4. Change **wing** to _____ wing

5. Change **lag** to _____ lag

6. Change **room** to _____ room

7. Change **rip** to _____ rip

8. Change **late** to _____ late

| d | s | b | t | p | f | g | c |

Name _____

Who Am I?

1. Cut out the letter blends at the bottom of the page.

2. Paste the letters to make a word.
Use the clues to help you.

3. Draw a picture to show what each word is.

---

1. Ssss. Here I come.

☐ ake

4. Buzz, buzz.

☐ y

2. Hop, hop. Splash!

☐ og

5. Look at my claws.

☐ ab

3. Hold your nose!

☐ unk

6. I have a long neck.

☐ an

| cr | fl | sn | sk | sw | fr |

Name _____

Picture Words

1. Say each picture name.

2. Put the words together.
   Now you have a new word.

3. Show what word it is.
   Cut and paste the pictures
   from the bottom of the page.

1.  + =

2. +  =

3. + =

4. + =

5. + =

Name _____

On the Chart

1. Say the picture names.
Listen for the beginning sounds.

2. Cut and paste the pictures
under the letters that stand
for those beginning sounds.

br	**st**	**cl**

Name _____

Picture Perfect

1. Say each picture name.
Listen for the beginning sound

2. Cut out the pictures at the bottom of the page.
Paste each picture in the right frame.
Use the clues to help you.

Clue

1. Begins like

2. Begins like

3. Begins like

4. Begins like

5. Begins like

Instant Phonics Practice © 1999, 2009 Linda Ward Beech, Scholastic Teaching Resources

Name _____

Slide the Letters

1. Cut out the pictures and the letter strips.

2. Cut out the slits on the pictures.

3. Slide the letter strips through the slits to make words.

4. Read the words.

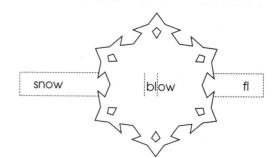

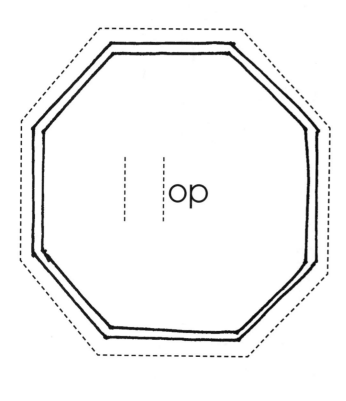

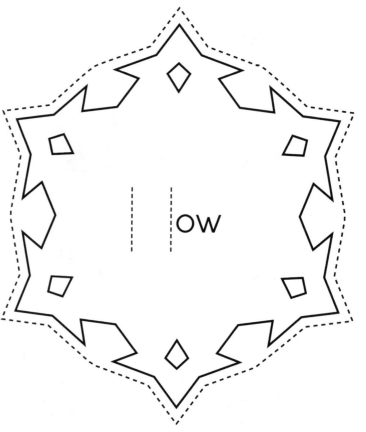

stop	st	cl	pl	dr	cr	fl
snow	sn	st	bl	gr	sl	fl

____-Blend Wheel Mini-Book

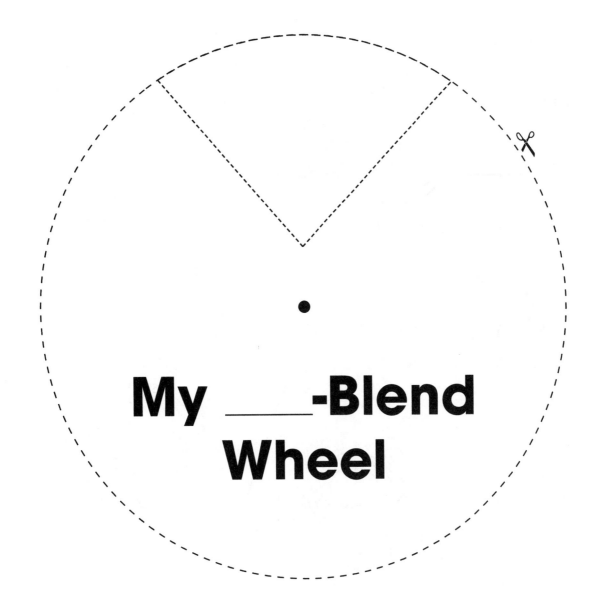

My ___-Blend Wheel

____-Blend Wheel Mini-Book

Wheel 1
(l-blends)

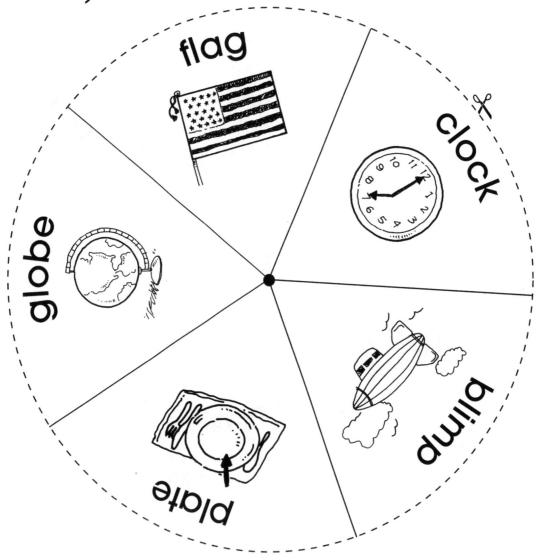

Instant Phonics Practice © 1999, 2009 Linda Ward Beech, Scholastic Teaching Resources

_____-Blend Wheel Mini-Book

Wheel 2
(r-blends)

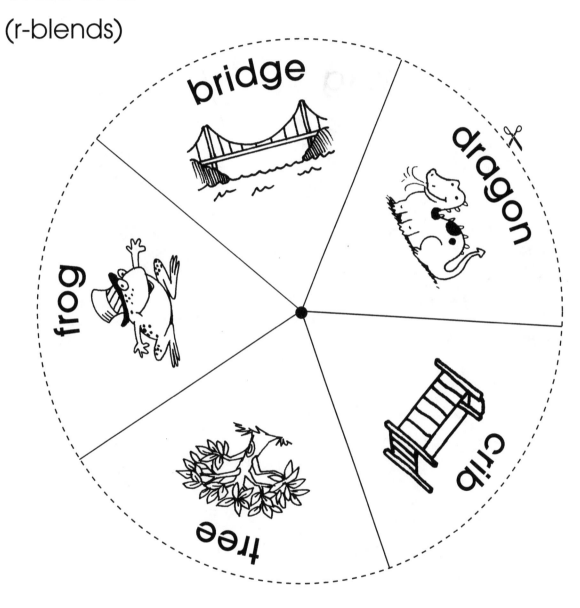

____-Blend Wheel Mini-Book

Wheel 3
(s-blends)

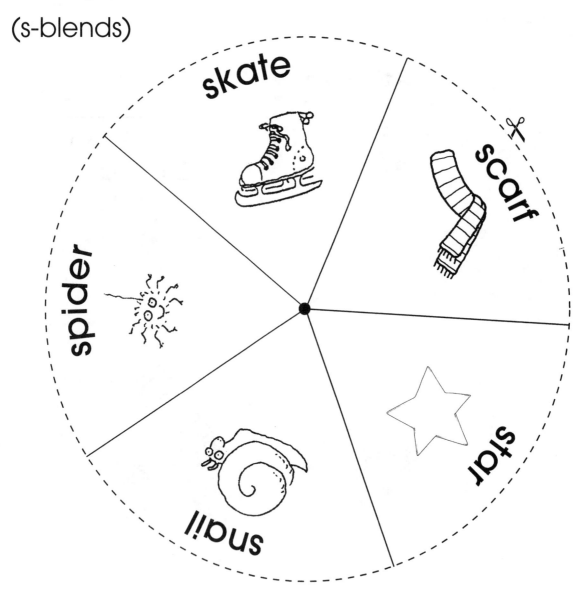

Instant Phonics Practice © 1999, 2009 Linda Ward Beech, Scholastic Teaching Resources

Name _____

Short Vowel Crosswords

Add a short vowel to make words in each puzzle.
Use the picture clues to help you.

1.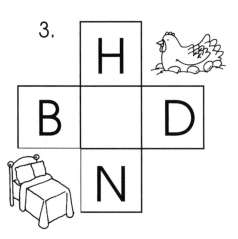

2.

3.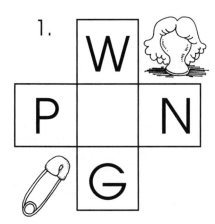

4.

5.

Name _____

Short Vowel Banners

1. Say the picture names at the bottom of the page.

2. Listen for the short-a sound, as in 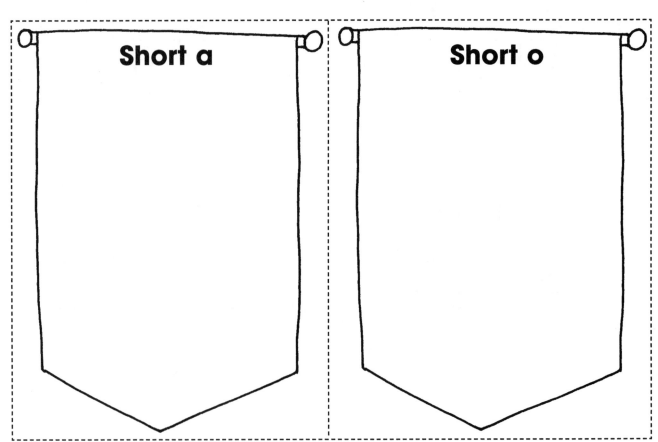.

Listen for the short-o sound, as in .

3. Cut out the pictures and the banners.

4. Cut and paste each picture on the banner with its vowel sound.

Short a

Short o

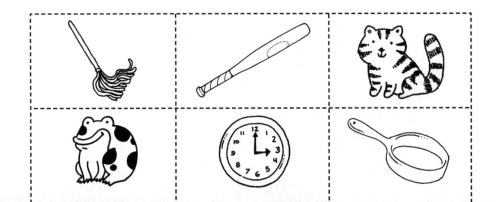

Instant Phonics Practice © 1999, 2009 Linda Ward Beech, Scholastic Teaching Resources

Name _____

Short Vowel Tic-Tac-Toe

1. Say the picture names in each grid.

2. Find and color 3 pictures in a row
that have the same short vowel sound.
Pictures can run across or up and down.

1. Short-a sound, as in
2. Short-i sound, as in

3. Short-e sound, as in

Name _____

Short Vowel Animals

1. Cut out the letters at the bottom of the page.

2. Paste each letter in the correct ⊓ so it spells the animal's name.

1. H___N

2. P___G

3. CR___B

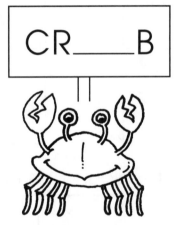

4. P___P

5. FR___G

I   O   A   E   U

Name _____

Bunny Hop

1. Cut out the pictures at the bottom of the page.
Also cut out Bunny and set aside.

2. Say the picture names.

3. Do you hear the short-u sound, as in "cut"?
If so, paste the pictures on the stones.

4. Help Bunny hop home on the stones.

Start

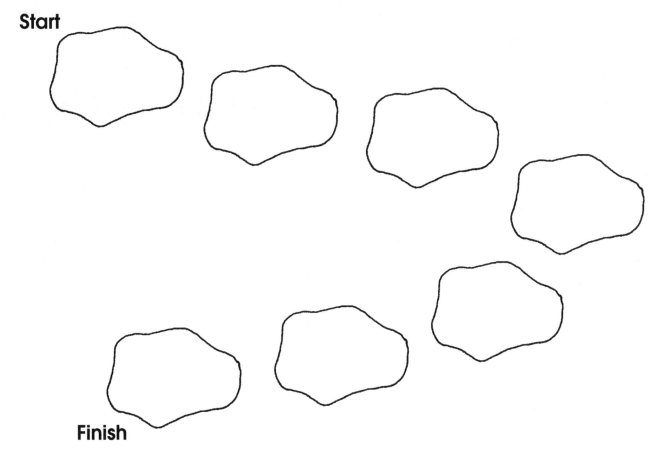

Finish

tab

Name _____

Letter Windows

1. Cut out the pictures and the letter strips.

2. Cut the slits on the pictures.

3. Slide the letter strips through the slits to make words.

4. Read the words.

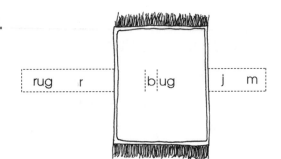

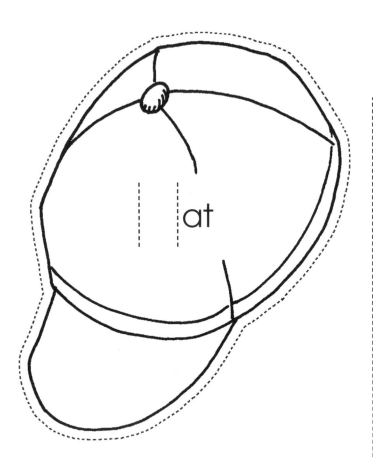

hat	h	f	c	s	m	p
rug	r	h	b	t	j	m

Instant Phonics Practice © 1999, 2009 Linda Ward Beech, Scholastic Teaching Resources

Name _____

Who Did It?

1. Who took the 🎩 ?

2. Use the code to find out. Write the words.

3. Then draw a picture to show who has the hat.

Code				
■ = short o	● = short a	▲ = short e	◆ = short u	◗ = short i

1. It is not the d ◆ ck. _____

2. It is not the c ● t. _____

3. It is not the p ◗ g. _____

4. Is it the f ■ x? _____

5. No, it is the h ▲ n. _____

6. She needs it for a n ▲ st. _____

Name _____

At the Shop

1. Say the picture names.

2. Listen for the short-e, short-i, and short-u vowel sounds.

3. Cut out the pictures at the bottom of the page. Paste each picture in the window that has the same vowel sound.

Short e   **Short i**   **Short u**

Instant Phonics Practice © 1999, 2009 Linda Ward Beech, Scholastic Teaching Resources

Name _____

Toss and Tell

Players: 1 or 2

1. Cut and paste the cube.
2. Toss the cube. Say the picture name on top.
3. Look at the word list. Make a ✓ next to each word that has the same vowel sound as the picture name.

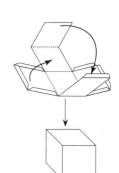

		Word List		
pig	top	sled	cab	egg
at	win	rug	hog	bug
hot	vest	ham	mud	hill

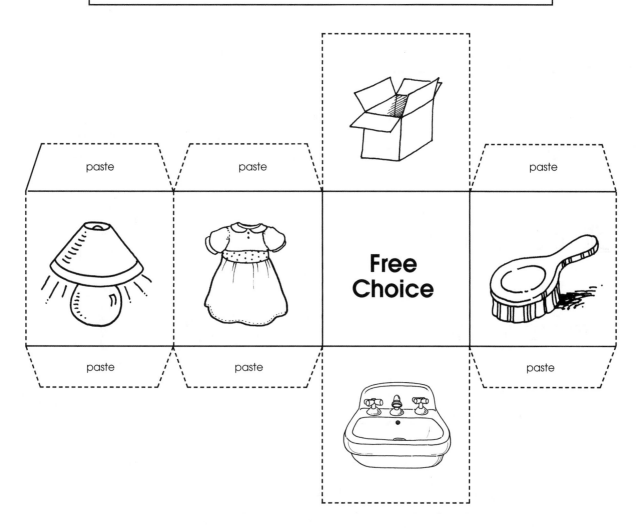

paste   paste

Free
Choice

paste

paste   paste

paste

Name _____

Sentence Fun

1. Look at the underlined words in each sentence.
   Say the vowel sound.

2. Find a word at the bottom of the page
   that has the same sound.

3. Does it make sense in the sentence?
   Use the clues to help you.

4. Finish the sentence.
   Cut and paste the words on the lines.

1. The <u>rat has</u> a _____.

2. <u>Ned fed</u> his _____.

3. The <u>duck</u> has <u>fun</u> in the _____.

4. <u>Did</u> the dog <u>tip</u> the _____?

5. Is the <u>man mad</u> or _____?

6. Did the <u>jet get</u> home _____?

yet	tub	hat
pet	dish	sad

Instant Phonics Practice © 1999, 2009 Linda Ward Beech, Scholastic Teaching Resources

Name _____

That Cat

1. Say the picture names at the bottom of the page.
Listen for the short vowel sounds.

2. Cut and paste the pictures into the correct boxes.
Use the clues to help you.

3. Cut out the cat.
Put it on the pictures as you read the sentences.

Clue

1. The cat is on a ⬜ .   short u

2. The cat is on a ⬜ .   short i

3. The cat is on a ⬜ .   short a

4. The cat is on a ⬜ .   short o

5. The cat is on a ⬜ .   short e

tab

What's in the Truck? Mini-Book

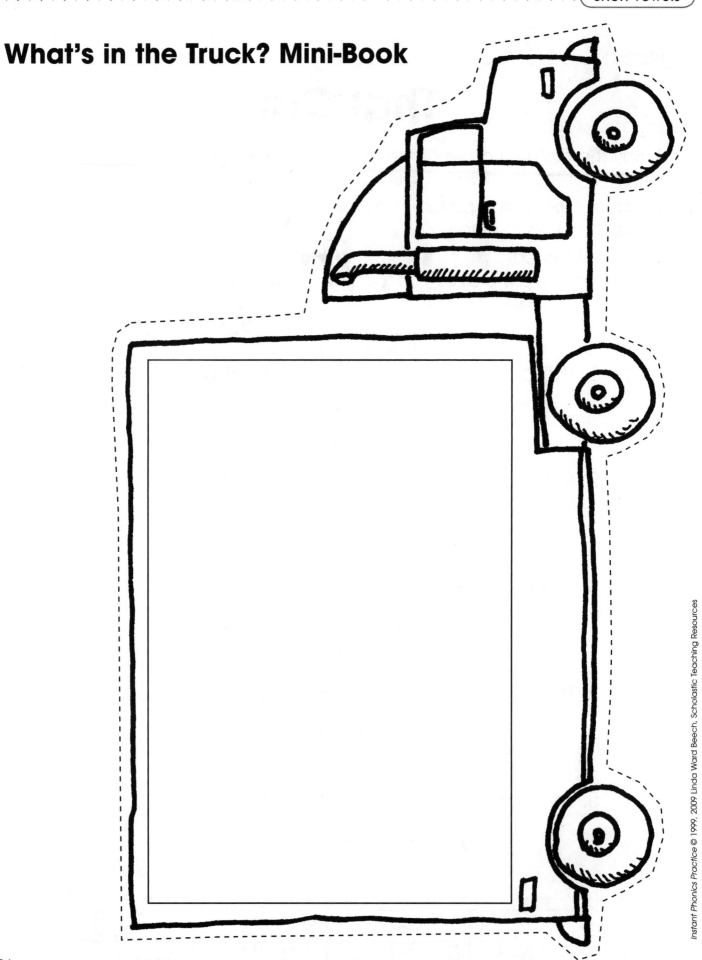

What's in the Truck?

Short a

My picture   1

Short e

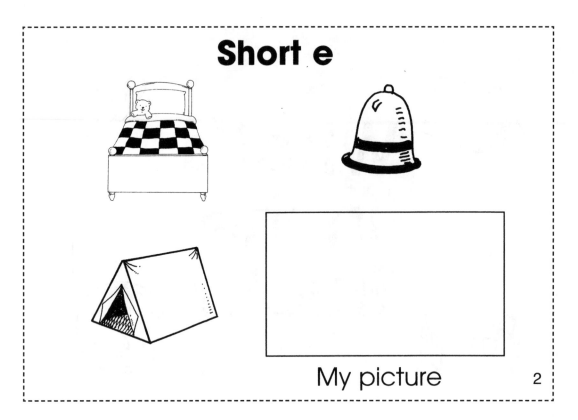

My picture 2

Short i

My picture 3

Instant Phonics Practice © 1999, 2009 Linda Ward Beech, Scholastic Teaching Resources

Short o

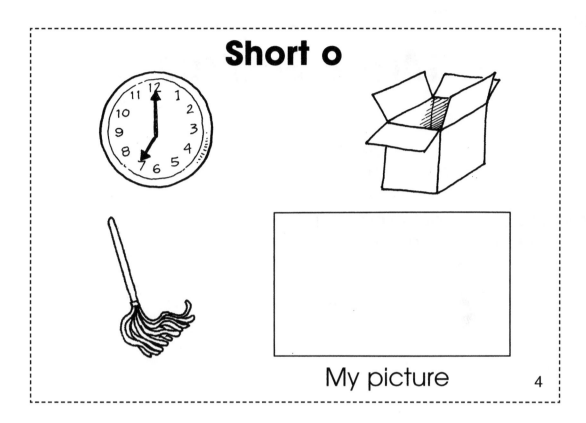

My picture

4

Short u

My picture

5

Instant Phonics Practice © 1999, 2009 Linda Ward Beech, Scholastic Teaching Resources

Name _____

Make Snakes

1. Say each picture name on the left.

2. Does the picture name have
the long-a sound, as in "snake"?

3. If so, cut out a snake body
from the bottom of the page.
Paste it to that snake's head.

 1.

 2.

 3.

 4.

 5.

 6.

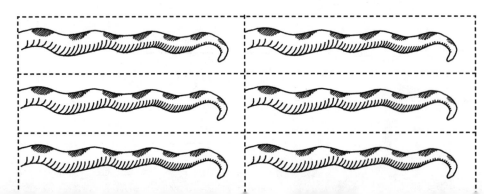

Instant Phonics Practice © 1999, 2009 Linda Ward Beech, Scholastic Teaching Resources

Name _____

Animal Crossword

1. Say the picture names.
Listen for the long vowel sound in each word.

2. Write the correct word for each picture in the boxes.
Use the Word Bank to help you.

Across

2. 　　6. 　　9. 　　11.

5. 　　7. 　　10.

Down

1.

2.

3.

4.

7.

8.

Word Bank

bee	ladybug	seal
deer	lion	sheep
eel	mole	snail
goat	mule	snake
jay		

Name _____

On the Tree

1. Say each picture name at the bottom of the page.

2. Do you hear the long-e sound, as in "tree"?
   If so, cut and paste the picture on the tree.

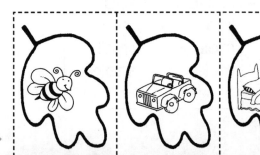

Name _____

Picture Maze

1. Make your way to the end of this maze!
   Begin by saying each picture name.

2. Listen for the sound of long a.

3. Color the picture if its name has the long-a sound.

Start

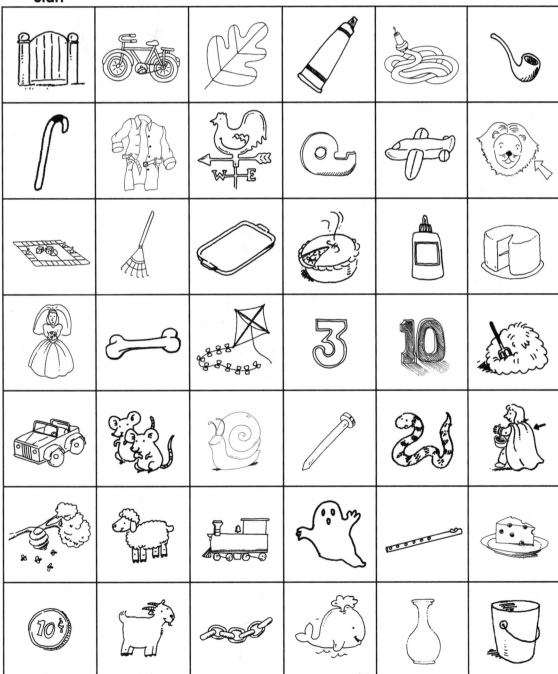

Finish

Name _____

Long-i Cut and Paste

1. Say each picture name at the bottom of the page.

2. Do you hear the long-i sound, as in "hive"?

3. If so, cut and paste the picture on the kite tail.

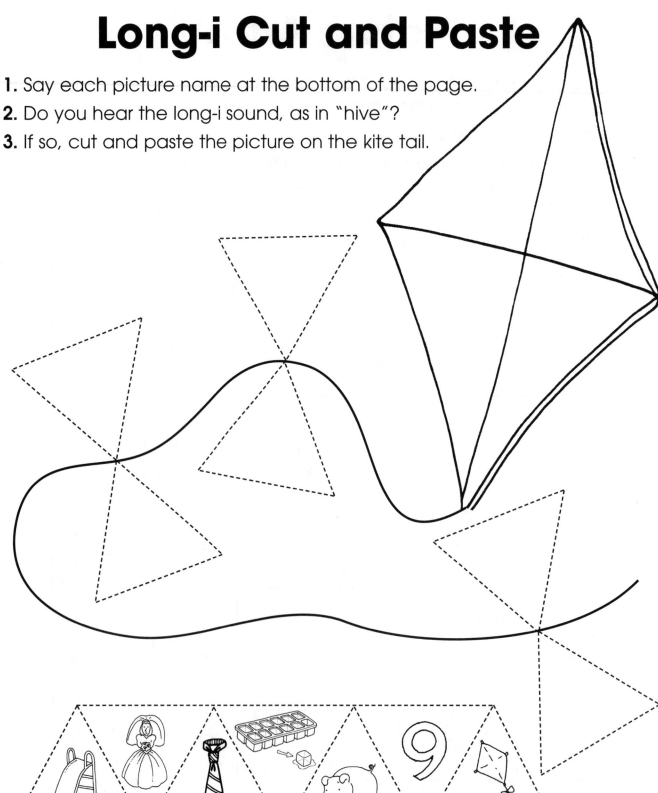

Name _____

Grid Game

1. Who hid in the grid? Find some of the animals.
Use the letter and number pairs in the 6 questions below.

2. Color those animals.

3. Say their names. Then write them on the lines.
What vowel sound do they share?

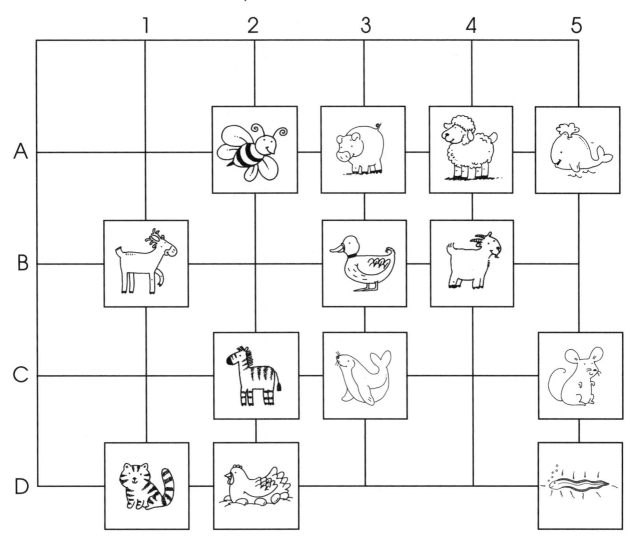

1. A, 2 _____   4. A, 4 _____

2. B, 1 _____   5. C, 3 _____

3. C, 2 _____   6. D, 5 _____

Name _____

Ghost Questions

1. Say each picture name at the bottom of the page.

2. Which ones have the long-o sound, as in 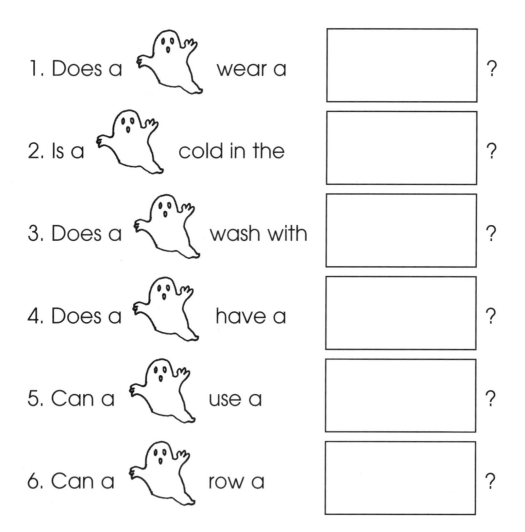?

3. Finish the questions. Cut and paste the long-o words into the correct boxes.

1. Does a 　　　　 wear a ☐ ?

2. Is a 　　　　 cold in the ☐ ?

3. Does a 　　　　 wash with ☐ ?

4. Does a 　　　　 have a ☐ ?

5. Can a 　　　　 use a ☐ ?

6. Can a 　　　　 row a ☐ ?

Name _____

U Stew

1. Cut out the pictures at the bottom of the page.
   Also cut open the slits on the pot.

2. Say the picture names.

3. Do you hear the long-u sound, as in "blue"?
   If so, slip the pictures into the stew.

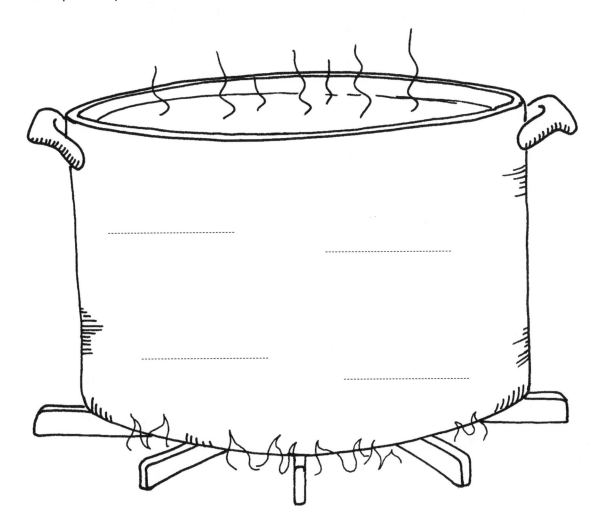

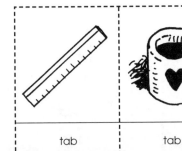

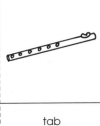

| tab | tab | tab | tab | tab | tab |

Name _____

Whale Tale

1. Say the picture names at the bottom of the page.
Listen for the long vowel sounds.

2. Cut and paste the pictures into the correct boxes.
Use the clues to help you.

3. Cut out the whale.
Help him swim by the pictures as you read the sentences.
Then tell a tale about your whale!

Clue

1. The whale likes [ ] .   long i

2. The whale meets a [ ] .   long e

3. The whale has a [ ] .   long o

4. The whale plays a [ ] .   long u

5. The whale sees a [ ] .   long a

tab

Name _____

Changes

1. Follow the clues to make new words.

2. Write each new word.

3. Cut out the pictures at the bottom of the page.
Paste each picture to show what the new word is.

Clues

1. Change **a** to **o**.   pale _____

2. Change **i** to **a**.   vine _____

3. Change **o** to **u**.   mole _____

4. Change **e** to **o**.   beat _____

5. Change **a** to **i**.   bake _____

6. Change **i** to **o**.   rise _____

Name _____

Riddle Fun

1. Write the word for each picture on the lines.
2. Then make a word that answers the riddle.
3. Use the letters in the boxes.

1. What kind of ball will not bounce? a _____ball

2. What flies without wings? _____

Instant Phonics Practice © 1999, 2009 Linda Ward Beech, Scholastic Teaching Resources

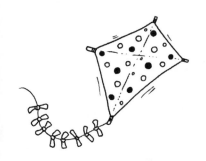

Colors
Around the Year

It's fall.

The leaves are

_____.

Hint: long o

Colors Around the Year Mini-Book, page 101

1

It's raining.

The sky is

_____.

Hint: long a

2

Instant Phonics Practice © 1999, 2009 Linda Ward Beech. Scholastic Teaching Resources

It's winter.

The snow is

_____.

Hint: long i

3

It's spring.

The grass is

_____.

Hint: long e

4

It's summer.

The sky is

_____.

Hint: long u

5

Colors Around the Year Mini-Book Word Strip

| green | gold | blue | gray | white |

Name _____

Wrong One Game

1. Say the picture names in each circle.
Listen for the vowel sound.

2. What picture name in each circle
doesn't share the same vowel sound?

3. Say the picture names at the bottom of the page.
Cut and paste pictures to replace the words that don't belong.

1.

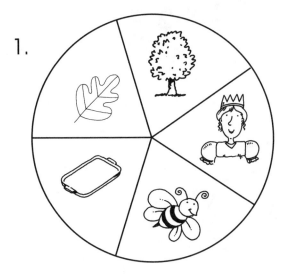

2.

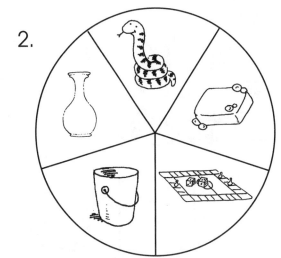

3.

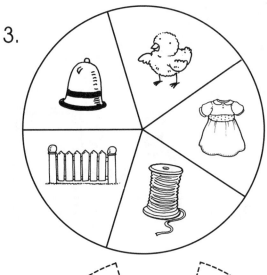

4.

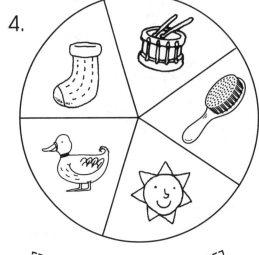

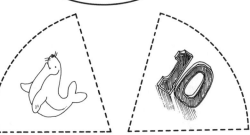

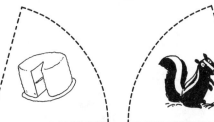

Name _____

Train Ride

1. One train picks up things with the long-a sound.
   The other picks up things with the short-a sound.

2. Say each picture name at the bottom of the page.
   Listen for the vowel sound.

3. Cut and paste pictures along the correct track.

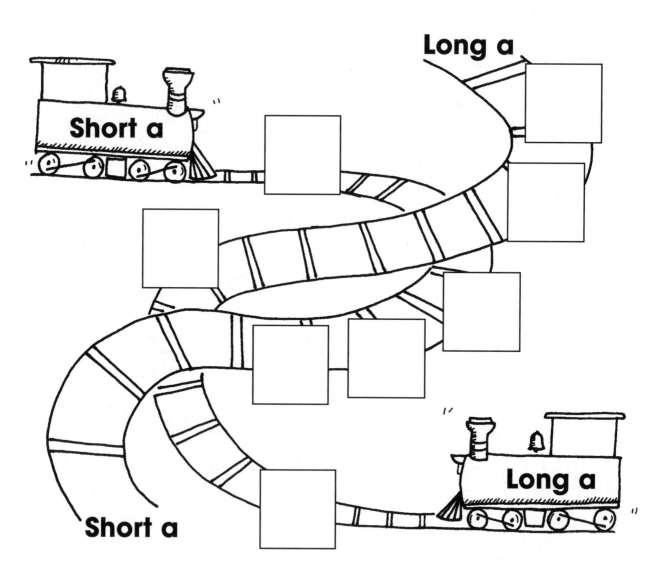

Instant Phonics Practice © 1999, 2009 Linda Ward Beech, Scholastic Teaching Resources

Name _____

What's Missing?

1. Something is missing from each picture.

2. Read the clues.

3. Look at the pictures to find out what it is.

4. Say the name of each missing item. Add it to the picture.

1.

Clue: long o
You drive on it.

2.

Clue: short a
You hit a ball with it.

3.

Clue: long e
You need two.

4.

Clue: short e
You sleep on it.

5.

Clue: long i
You fly it.

Name _____

Short and Long

1. Say each picture name at the bottom of the page.

2. Cut and paste the picture next to the word pair that has its name.

3. Circle the correct word for each picture.

1. van
   vane

2. cube
   cub

3. pine
   pin

4. cape
   cap

5. tub
   tube

6. rob
   robe

7. cane
   can

8. mope
   mop

Instant Phonics Practice © 1999, 2009 Linda Ward Beech, Scholastic Teaching Resources

Name _____

Name the Vowels

Players: 1 or 2

1. Cut out the wheel.

2. Make a spinner using a ⬭ and a ✏.

3. Spin. Say the picture name the spinner lands on.

4. Name the vowel sound you hear.
Tell if it is long or short.

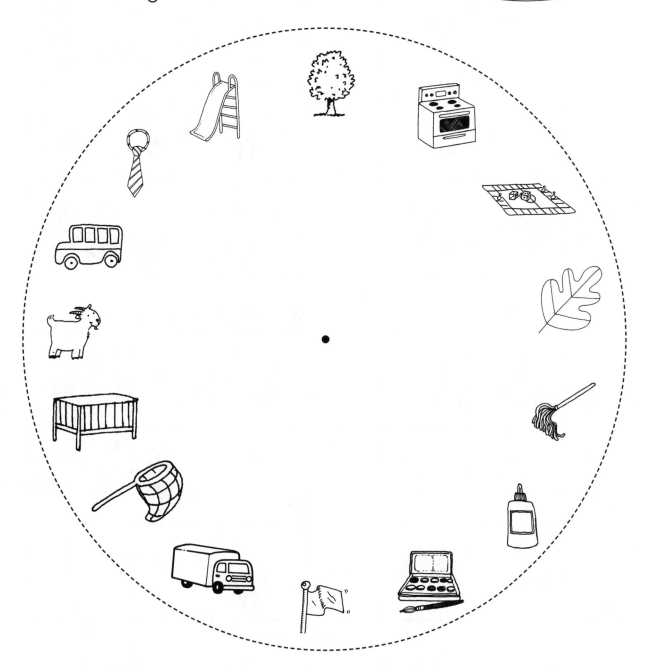

Name _____

Vowel Tic-Tac-Toe

1. Say the picture names in each grid.

2. Find and color 3 pictures in a row that have the same vowel sound.

1. Short-e sound

2. Long-i sound

3. Short-u sound

4. Long-o sound

Instant Phonics Practice © 1999, 2009 Linda Ward Beech, Scholastic Teaching Resources

Name _____

Road Race Game

Players: 2

1. Cut out the cars.

2. Take turns tossing a penny.
- If it lands 🪙, move 1 space.
- If it lands 🪙, move 2 spaces.

3. Name the vowel sound. Is it long or short?

4. The car to reach Finish first wins.

Start

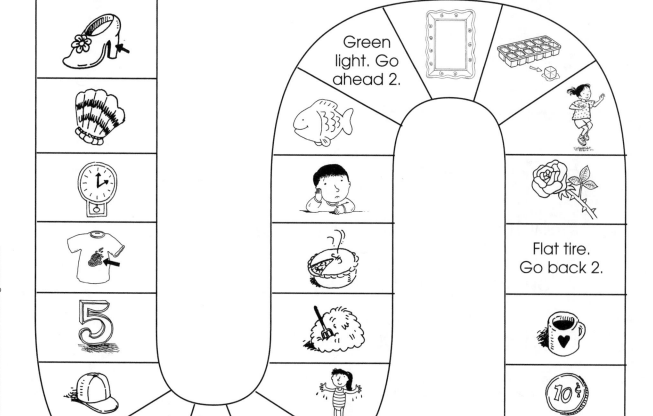

Green light. Go ahead 2.

Flat tire. Go back 2.

Stop for gas. Miss a turn.

Finish

Name _____

Vowel Opposites

1. Read each word.

2. Use the clues to help you write its opposite.

Clue	Word	Opposite
1. short i	out	_____
2. long a	work	_____
3. short u	open	_____
4. short o	cold	_____
5. long u	me	_____
6. short a	glad	_____
7. long e	wake	_____
8. long i	black	_____
9. long o	stop	_____
10. short e	women	_____

Instant Phonics Practice © 1999, 2009 Linda Ward Beech, Scholastic Teaching Resources

Name _____

Number Match-Up

1. Say the number words at the bottom of the page. Listen for the vowel sound in each word.

2. Cut and paste the word under the correct picture.

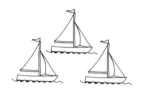

1. The number is

_____.

(Hint: long e)

2. The number is

_____.

(Hint: long i)

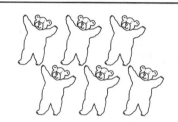

3. The number is

_____.

(Hint: short i)

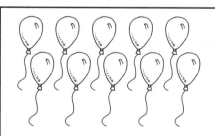

4. The number is

_____.

(Hint: short e)

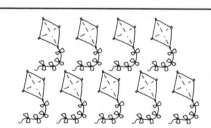

5. The number is

_____.

(Hint: long i)

five | three | nine | ten | six

Name _____

Color Clues

1. Say the words at the bottom of the page.
Listen for the vowel sound in each word.

2. Cut and paste the words into the correct boxes.
Use the clues to help you.

 1. The color is
(Hint: short a)

 2. The color is
(Hint: short i)

 3. The color is
(Hint: long e)

 4. The color is
(Hint: long u)

 5. The color is
(Hint: short e)

 6. The color is
(Hint: long a)

blue ┆ pink ┆ green ┆ red ┆ gray ┆ black

Instant Phonics Practice © 1999, 2009 Linda Ward Beech, Scholastic Teaching Resources

Going to Work

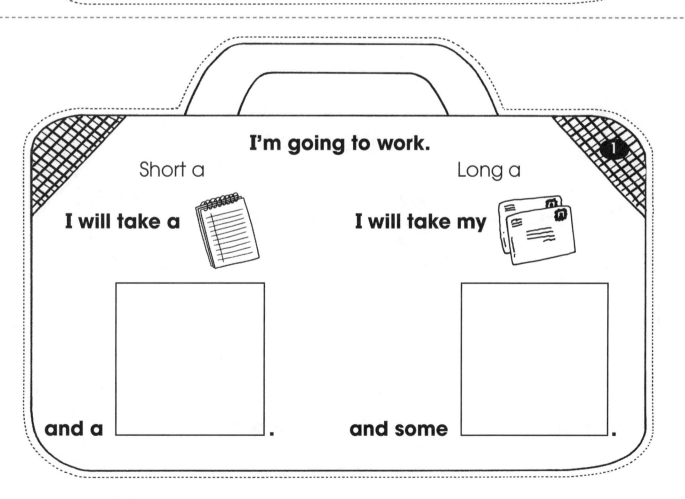

I'm going to work.

Short a   Long a

I will take a   I will take my

and a   .   and some   .

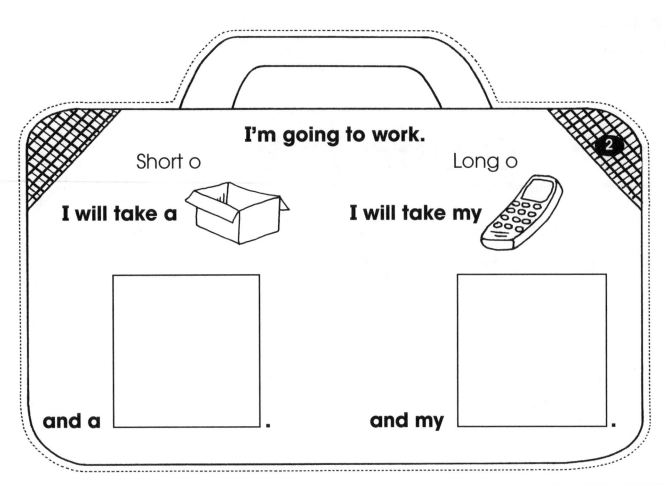

I'm going to work.

②

Short o

Long o

I will take a

I will take my

and a [ ] .

and my [ ] .

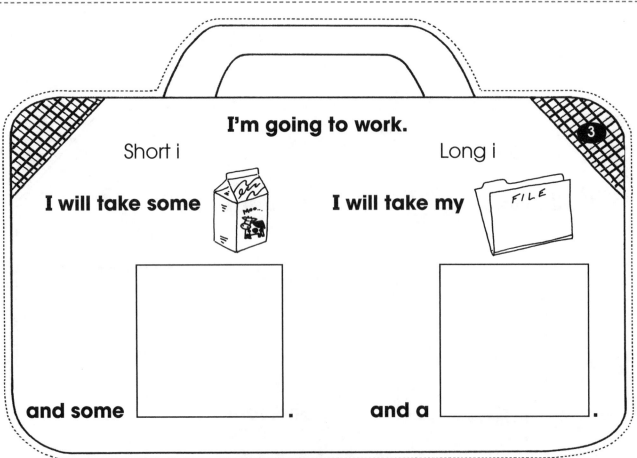

I'm going to work.

③

Short i

Long i

I will take some

I will take my

FILE

and some [ ] .

and a [ ] .

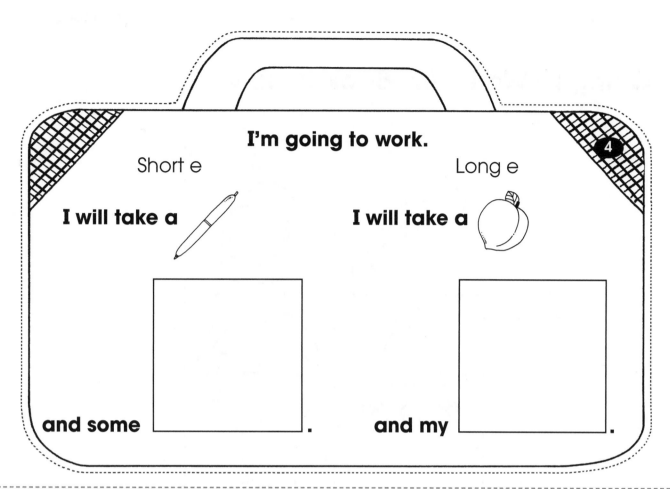

I'm going to work.

Short e   Long e

I will take a   **I will take a**

and some ☐ .   **and my** ☐ .

④

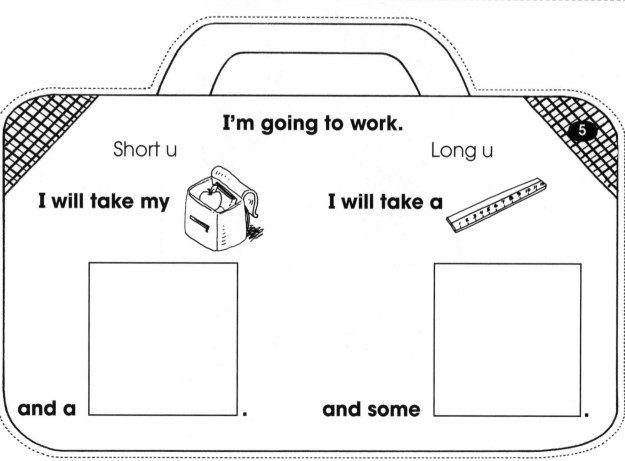

I'm going to work.

Short u   Long u

I will take my   **I will take a**

and a ☐ .   **and some** ☐ .

⑤

Going to Work Mini-Book Pictures

Instant Phonics Practice © 1999, 2009 Linda Ward Beech. Scholastic Teaching Resources

Name _____

Rhymes and Shapes

1. Say the words.

2. Cut out the shapes at the bottom of the page.

3. Complete each shape. Paste each word
next to a word it rhymes with.

1. sack

2. wet

3. pot

4. kid

5. bump

6. map

tap   lid   get   hot   back   pump

Name _____

Word Family Flowers

1. Say the picture name on each flower.

2. Say the picture names on the petals.

    • Which words rhyme with 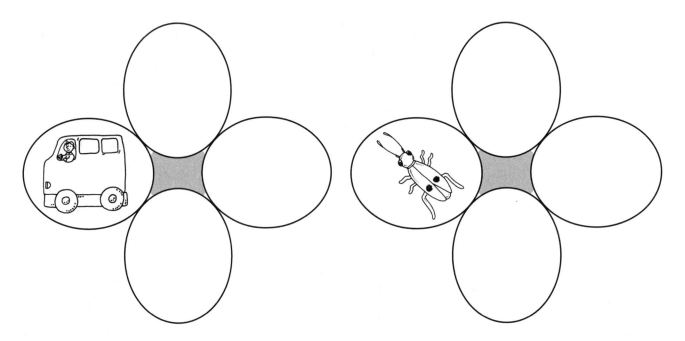?

    • Which words rhyme with ?

3. Cut and paste the petals on the correct flower.

Instant Phonics Practice © 1999, 2009 Linda Ward Beech, Scholastic Teaching Resources

Name _____

Rhyme Roll Game

Players: 2

1. Take turns rolling a penny on the game board.

2. Say the word the penny lands on.

3. Think of two words that rhyme with that word.

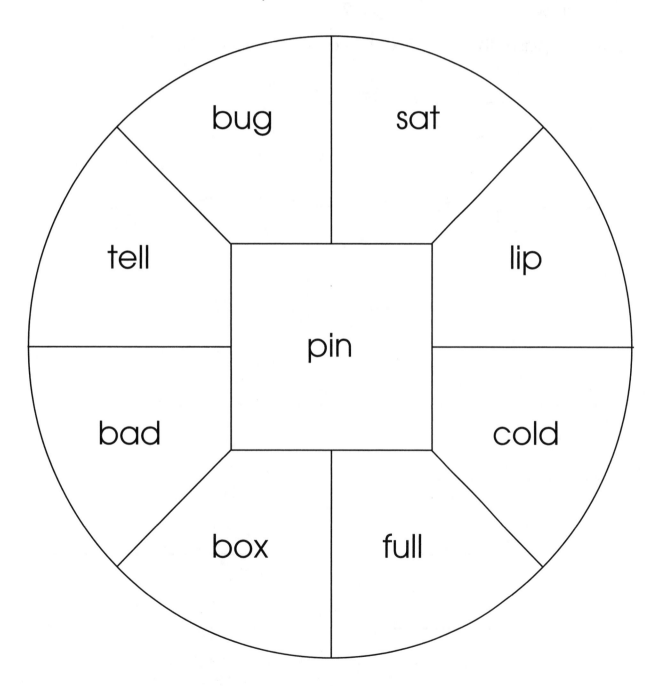

Name _____

Words on a Web

1. Cut out the letters at the bottom of the page.

2. Make new words that end with –**it**.

3. Paste the letters on the web.

4. Write the words on the lines.

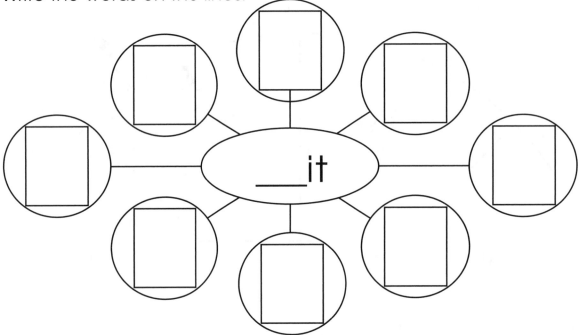

1. _____   5. _____

2. _____   6. _____

3. _____   7. _____

4. _____   8. _____

| p | h | s | l | b | f | k | w |

Instant Phonics Practice © 1999, 2009 Linda Ward Beech, Scholastic Teaching Resources

Name _____

Fat Cat Game

Players: 2

1. Start with number 1.
Think of 2 short-a words that rhyme—like **fat cat**.

2. The other player tries to guess the letters in the words.

3. For each new correct letter, draw 1 part of the cat.

4. Take turns using different short vowels.
How many cats can you make?

Write the letters on the lines.

1. short a
   rhyme ___ ___ ___   ___ ___ ___

2. short e
   rhyme ___ ___ ___   ___ ___ ___

3. short o
   rhyme ___ ___ ___   ___ ___ ___

4. short i
   rhyme ___ ___ ___   ___ ___ ___

5. short u
   rhyme ___ ___ ___   ___ ___ ___

Name _____

Rhyme Flip-Ups

1. Say the picture names at the bottom of the page.

2. Then read the words in the boxes.

3. Cut and paste the tab on each picture
above the word it rhymes with.

4. Think of more rhyming words.
Make new flip-up pages.
Add them to the ones below.

1. | paste |
|---|
wag
bag

2. | paste |
|---|
yell
tell

3. | paste |
|---|
fun
run

4. | paste |
|---|
red
led

5. | paste |
|---|
win
tin

6. | paste |
|---|
fuss
us

tab	tab	tab	tab	tab	tab

Rhyme Find

1. Say each picture name.
2. Which picture name at the bottom of the page rhymes with the picture names in each row?
3. Cut and paste the pictures into the correct boxes.

1.

2.

3.

4.

5.

Name _____

Rhyme Hunt

1. Do the word search puzzle below.
Find and circle the 5 words from each Word Bank.
Words can go across and down.

2. Then write the words on a sheet of paper.

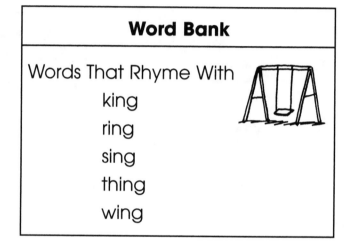

Word Bank
Words That Rhyme With hide ride side tide wide

Word Bank
Words That Rhyme With king ring sing thing wing

```
T H I N G K J X
W I N G B I U H
A D O S I N G L
F E C L Y G Z T
S J R I N G A I
I R I D E M V D
D T K E W I D E
E A P V H C X T
```

Instant Phonics Practice © 1999, 2009 Linda Ward Beech, Scholastic Teaching Resources

Name _____

Silly Sock Rhymes

1. Read the word on each sock at the bottom of the page.

2. Find a sock on the line that has a word that rhymes.

3. Match up the socks that have words that rhyme.

4. Cut and paste the socks next to each other to make a pair.

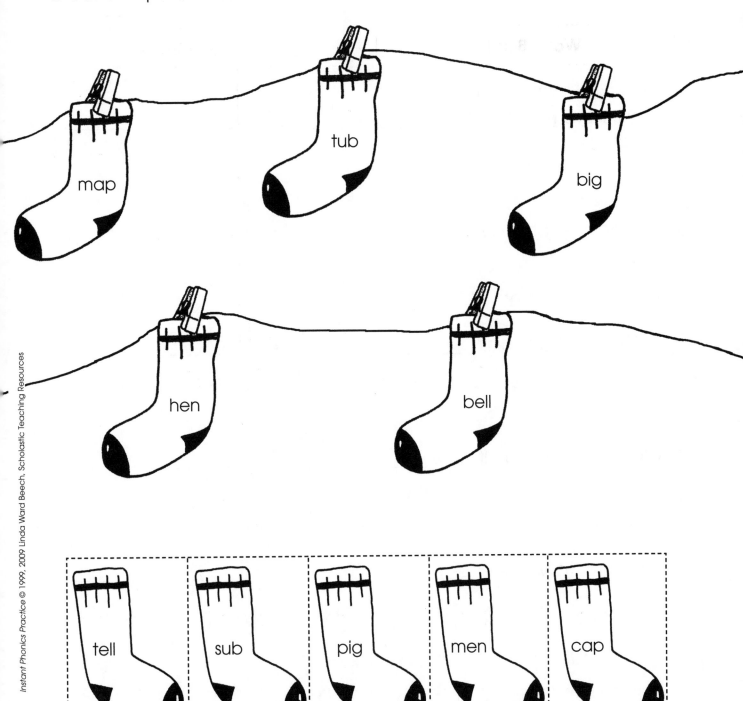

Name _____

Make It Rhyme

1. Look at the underlined word in each sentence.

2. Find a rhyming word at the bottom of the page.

3. Cut and paste it at the end of the sentence.

4. Draw a picture for each rhyme.

1. Can Jake <u>ride</u> down the _____?

2. We can <u>each</u> have a _____.

3. Let's <u>meet</u> on Main _____.

4. What do you <u>say</u> in the _____?

5. <u>Sue</u> likes to wear _____.

Instant Phonics Practice © 1999, 2009 Linda Ward Beech, Scholastic Teaching Resources

| peach | street | play | slide | blue |

Cut out the pictures. Paste them on the pages of your book.

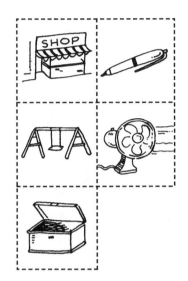

Rhyme Time

Rhyme Time Mini-Book, page 127

What did Pop do with the mop?

What did Ben get from the men?

He got a hen and

a ___ ___ ___.

Instant Phonics Practice © 1999, 2009 Linda Ward Beech, Scholastic Teaching Resources

What did Jan pack in the van?

She packed a pan and

a ___ ___ ___.

1

Rhyme Time Mini-Book, page 128

Sop, flop, slop around

the ___ ___ ___ ___!

6

What did Bing bring to the king?

Instant Phonics Practice © 1999, 2009 Linda Ward Beech, Scholastic Teaching Resources

A ring, some string, and

a ___ ___ ___ ___.

3

What did Skunk put on his bunk?

Some junk that stunk and

his ___ ___ ___ ___.

4